COLUMBIA

# 1 0 0 0

# WORDS YOU

# MUST KNOW

# for GRE®

**BOOK ONE WITH ANSWERS**

## Richard Lee, Ph.D.

COLUMBIA PRESS

*All inquiries should be addressed to:*

Columbia Press International

803-470 Granville Street

Vancouver, BC  V6C 1V5

Email: richardleephd@hotmail.com

ISBN-13：978-1-927647-17-2

To Nancy, Philip, and Christina

# CONTENTS

---

ambivalent, pungent, solvent, indent, prevalent
ameliorate, conglomerate, degenerate, intoxicate, retaliate

audacious, capacious, loquacious, rapacious, sagacious
auspicious, vicious, judicious, malicious, officious

behemoth, broth, moth, sloth, wroth
boisterous, grievous, raucous, zealous, sumptuous

bombast, blast, aghast, forecast, iconoclast
burlesque, grotesque, picturesque, sculpturesque, statuesque

burnish, anguish, furnish, garnish, tarnish
burrow, billow, escrow, marrow, shallow

congeal, heal, appeal, conceal, ordeal
contentious, abstentious, licentious, pretentious, sententious

contravene, gene, hygiene, obscene, serene
converge, merge, diverge, emerge, submerge

copious, dubious, odious, commodious, mischievous
corroborate, expurgate, promulgate, affiliate, exaggerate

culpable, blamable, censurable, reproachable, unbearable
cursory, mandatory, promissory, conservatory, observatory

deplete, concrete, discrete, replete, obsolete
discrepancy, chancy, fancy, necromancy, sycophancy

efface, disgrace, retrace, aerospace, interface
elucidate, abate, conflate, rebate, stagnate

enigmatic, phlegmatic, pragmatic, traumatic, charismatic
eschew, shrew, curfew, overview, purview

fallible, feasible, eligible, imperceptible, intelligible
foreboding, cling, fling, offspring, uprising

forensic, hectic, heretic, lunatic, diplomatic

# TO THE STUDENT

The shortest and best way of learning a language is to know the roots of it, that is, those original primitive words from which other words are formed.

-- Lord Chesterfield

**Columbia 1000 Words You Must Know for GRE** presents 1000 most frequently tested words for GRE. You will find 100 vocabulary-building lessons in Books 1 – 3. Each lesson contains 10 new words and they are first presented to you with **Memory Tips**; next, **New Words** are listed in rhyming memory groups and followed by **Sample Sentences**; the last part of the lesson are **Sentence Completion** and **Definition Matching** practice tests with answers. One of the most outstanding features of this book is that each new word is repeated at least five times in a lesson so that you will have a much better chance to memorize it more easily.

**Columbia 1000 Words You Must Know for GRE** is designed to help you master all the absolutely essential GRE words using our most effective memory method: **A Roots and Rhyming Memory Approach**. Let's take the word "**aberration**" for example and see how this exciting new memory method can help you find the shortest and best way to memorize new words and build a large vocabulary:

1. **MEMORY TIPS:** Memorizing words with the help of Roots, Prefixes, and Suffixes.

   *ion*       condition or action; as ***aberration***, *ration, inflation, temptation, abbreviation*

2. **NEW WORDS:** New Words are arranged in rhyming groups for easy memory.

| aberration | ration | inflation | temptation | abbreviation |
|------------|--------|-----------|------------|--------------|

ABERRATION[ˌæbəˈreɪʃ(ə)n]*n.* departure from what is right or true  **rhyming sound – ation**

3. **SAMPLE SENTENCES:** Sample Sentences are given to help you memorize words in context.

*This complexity is not an **aberration** or something to be wished away, it is the new reality.*

4. **SENTENCE COMPLETION:** Sentence Completion is designed to help you memorize words through tests.

*The patient's only _____ was a temporary lapse of memory. (**aberration**)*

5. **DEFINITION MATCHING:** Definition Matchingis designed to help you memorize words through repetition.

*departure from what is right or true_____ (**aberration**)*

In this example, the repeated appearance of the word "**aberration**" in the lesson makes it easy for you to memorize. Therefore you can see that only by repeated practice or reinforcement of a new word under different circumstances can you really memorize it so unconsciously that you will never forget. Human memory, like the unconscious, is structured like a language. Once you have memorized a new word, it will stay in your unconscious and become part of yourself. Whenever you need it, it will come to you automatically just like the flowers coming in the spring: it is natural!

**Columbia 1000 Words You Must Know for GRE** is both a self-help book and a textbook for classroom use. It is the only vocabulary book you will ever need to master the most often tested words on the GRE. If you can spend about 25 minutes a day with this book, you will definitely help yourself expand your vocabulary, build up your word power, and raise your score on the GRE.

**Richard Lee, Ph.D.**

**Beautiful Vancouver**

# UNIT 1

## MEMORY TIPS:

Word building with Roots, Prefixes, and Suffixes:

---

| | |
|---|---|
| **ab** | way from, off; as *aback, aberration, abbreviation* |
| **in** | not; as *inflation* |
| **ion** | condition or action; as *ration, inflation, temptation, aberration, abbreviation* |
| **counter** | against; as *counterattack* |

---

## NEW WORDS

| aback | crack | rack | ransack | counterattack |
|---|---|---|---|---|
| aberration | ration | inflation | temptation | abbreviation |

**1. ABACK**  [ə'bæk] *adv.* surprised; startled  **rhyming sound -ack**

The finance minister admitted being taken **aback** by the scale of recent write-downs in the banking sector.

**2. crack**  [kræk] *v.* to break or split partially; to solve a problem; *n.* narrow gap

The scientist finally **cracked** the system after years of research.

**3. rack**  [ræk] *n.* framework for holding articles; *v.* to make someone suffer

The country is now **racked** by crimes and the violent separatist movement.

**4. ransack**  ['ræn,sæk] *v.* to go through a place stealing or damaging things

Some also fear that the Asian car maker will **ransack** Volvo's intellectual property to boost its less sophisticated cars.

**5. counterattack** ['kaʊntərə,tæk] *n.* attack made in response to an attack; *v.* to deliver a retaliatory attack

After the revolt spread, the General's forces rallied behind tanks and airpower and launched a fierce **counterattack**.

**6. ABERRATION** [ˌæbə'reɪʃ(ə)n] *n.* departure from what is right or true   **rhyming**

**sound -ation**

This complexity is not an **aberration** or something to be wished away, it is the new reality.

*Word Families*: **aberrant** *adj.*

**7. ration** ['ræʃ(ə)n] *n.* a limit amount of something; *v.* to control the supply of

The meat **ration** was down to one pound per person per week when the war broke out.

**8. inflation** [in'fleɪʃ(ə)n] *n.* increase in prices and fall in the value of money

In a single year, the **inflation** rate in this country has shot up from 30% to 45%.

**9. temptation** [temp'teɪʃ(ə)n] *n.* a strong feeling of wanting to have or do something

Man can almost resist anything except the **temptation** of money.

*Word Families*: **temptatious** *adj.*

**10. abbreviation** [ə,brivi'eɪʃ(ə)n] *n.* a short form of word or phrase

UNESCO is the **abbreviation** for United Nations Educational, Scientific and Cultural Organization.

*Word Families*: **abbreviate** *v.*; **abbreviative** *adj.*

# SENTENCE COMPLETION

Choose one of the new words to complete each sentence below. Make changes if necessary.

COLUMBIA 1000 WORDS YOU MUST KNOW FOR GRE

| aback | crack | rack | ransack | counterattack |
|-------|-------|------|---------|---------------|
| aberration | ration | inflation | temptation | abbreviation |

1. The thief got into Mary's apartment and began to _____ anything he could get his hands on.

2. The police are beginning to _____ down on drivers who speed near the school.

3. Joan is worried about her figure as she can't resist the _____ of chocolate and ice cream.

4. There was a grave food shortage in Anatolia , and bread was put on _____.

5. Every country is trying hard to tighten up its monetary policy to tamp down _____.

6. The woman was taken _____ by her children's opposition to her remarriage to an American millionaire.

7. He was on the _____ during the entire interview for the position of a private bodyguard for a famous Hollywood actress.

8. The patient's only _____ was a temporary lapse of memory.

9. SUNY is the _____ for the State University of New York.

10. After preparing for about a month, we finally launched a _____ against the enemies.


# DEFINITION MATCHING

Choose one of the new words to match each definition below.

| aback | crack | rack | ransack | counterattack |
|-------|-------|------|---------|---------------|
| aberration | ration | inflation | temptation | abbreviation |

11. departure from what is right or true _____

12. to break or split partially _____

13. a short form of word or phrase _____

14. to make someone suffer  _____

15. surprised; startled  _____

16. to go through a place damaging things  _____

17. a strong feeling of wanting to do something  _____

18. a limit amount of something  _____

19. to deliver a retaliatory attack against  _____

20. increase in prices and fall in the value of money  _____

# WRITING SENTENCES

Use each new word in the box to write an original sentence.

| aback | crack | rack | ransack | counterattack |
|-------|-------|------|---------|---------------|
| aberration | ration | inflation | temptation | abbreviation |

21. _____

22. _____

23. _____

24. _____

25. _____

26. _____

27. _____

28. _____

29. _____

30. _____

# UNIT 2

## MEMORY TIPS:

Word building with Roots, Prefixes, and Suffixes:

---

| | |
|---|---|
| **a, ab** | from, away; as *abet, asset, abhor* |
| **be** | make, cause, affect; as *beget* |
| **or** | one who; as *mentor; ambassador* |
| **re** | back, again; as *regret* |

---

## NEW WORDS

| | | | | |
|---|---|---|---|---|
| abet | asset | beget | cadet | regret |
| abhor | decor | mentor | metaphor | ambassador |

**1. ABET**     [əˈbet] *v.* to assist or encourage in crime or wrongdoing     **rhyming sound –et**

It is illegal to aid and **abet** a criminal.

*Word Families*: **abetment or abettal** *n.*; **abettor or abetter** *n.*

**2. asset**     [ˈæset] *n,.* anything valuable or useful

By the end of 2012 the company had **assets** of 35 billion dollars.

**3. beget**     [bɪˈget] *v.* to father; to cause or create

The only recognized purpose of their marriage was to **beget** children to help with the family's dairy farm.

**4. cadet**  [kə'dɛt] *n.* a young person who is training to be a police officer or military officer

After graduation from Columbia College, Jordon became a West Point **cadet**.

**5. regret**  [rɪ'grɛt] *v.* to feel sorry, repentant, or upset about; *n.* a sense of repentance or sorrow

We **regret** to say that your proposal is absolutely unacceptable to us.

Word Families: **regretful** *adj.;* **regretfully** *adv.;* **regrettable** *adj.*

**6. ABHOR**  [əb'hɔr] *v.* to hate; to detest          **rhyming sound –or**

We should **abhor** any form of racism.

**7. decor**  [deɪ'kɔr] *n.* a style or scheme of interior decoration, furnishings as in a room or house

The **decor** of the penthouse includes furniture of natural woods or bleached oaks imported from Italy.

**8. mentor**  ['mɛntər] *n.* a wise or trusted adviser or guide

Kennedy was a **mentor** during his early days in the United States Senate, and was an early and avid booster of his presidential campaign.

**9. metaphor**  ['mɛtə,fɔr] *n.* a figure of speech in which a word or phrase is applied to an object or action that it does not literally denote in order to imply a resemblance

The famous venture capitalist often tells startups to "skate where the puck is going" as a **metaphor** for thinking about where the future lies and planning for that now.

*Word Families*: **metaphorical** *adj.;* **metaphorically** *adv.*

**10. ambassador**  [æm'bæsədər] *n.* a diplomatic minister of the highest rank, accredited as the representative to another country or sovereign

The US **ambassador** to the UN, Susan Rice, said China was ready to hold "serious" talks with Western powers on a new UN resolution.

# SENTENCE COMPLETION

Choose one of the new words to complete each sentence below. Make changes if necessary.

| abet | asset | beget | cadet | regret |
|------|-------|-------|-------|--------|
| abhor | decor | mentor | metaphor | ambassador |

1. I _____ the assembly of evildoers and refuse to sit with the wicked.

2. Jenny's travels around the world has greatly influenced her _____ at home.

3. The _____ was giving a dinner for a few people whom he wished to talk to.

4. The criminal was aided and _____ by his girl friend

5. He is just a space _____, it looks like his dreams have never come true.

6. He would find it ironic that I see him as a _____ as, after working with him, I quit law.

7. As a matter of fact, economic tensions usually _____ political ones.

8. Being able to practice a trade is really an _____ in times of difficulties.

9. The Great Wall, and the sense of incomprehension that goes with it, also stands as a _____ for global investors' current worries.

10. She didn't _____ what she has said but felt that she could have expressed it differently.

# DEFINITION MATCHING

Choose one of the new words to match each definition below.

| abet | asset | beget | cadet | regret |
|------|-------|-------|-------|--------|
| abhor | decor | mentor | metaphor | ambassador |

11. a style or scheme of interior decoration _____

12. to feel sorry, repentant, or upset about _____

13. figure of speech to imply a resemblance     _____

14. to hate; to detest     _____

15. diplomatic minister to another country     _____

16. one in training to be a police or military officer     _____

17. to father; to cause or create     _____

18. a wise or trusted adviser or guide     _____

19. to assist or encourage in crime or wrongdoing     _____

20. anything valuable or useful     _____

# WRITING SENTENCES

Use each new word in the box to write an original sentence.

| abet | asset | beget | cadet | regret |
|------|-------|-------|-------|--------|
| abhor | decor | mentor | metaphor | ambassador |

21._____

22._____

23._____

24._____

25._____

26._____

27._____

28._____

29._____

30._____

# UNIT 3

## MEMORY TIPS:

Word building with Roots, Prefixes, and Suffixes:

---

| | |
|---|---|
| **ab** | from, away**;** as *abide, abject, affect* |
| **con** | together; as *confide* |
| **de** | from, away, reverse, against; as *defect* |
| **sub** | under; as *subside* |

---

## NEW WORDS

| | | | | |
|---|---|---|---|---|
| abide | collide | confide | subside | homicide |
| abject | affect | defect | neglect | prospect |

**1. ABIDE**  [əˈbaɪd] *v.* to remain; to put up with   **rhyming sound – ide**

If you join our club, you have to **abide** by our rules.

*Word Families*: **abidance** *n.*; **abiding** *adj.*

**2. collide**  [kəˈlaɪd] *v,.* to crash into each other

Two cars **collided** head-on on West Pender Street early this morning.

*Word Families*: **collision** *n.*

**3. confide**  [kənˈfaɪd] *v.* to tell someone a secret; to talk about your private feelings

Nowadays children seldom **confide** to their parents about what they think.

*Word Families*: **confidant** *n*.; **confident** *adj*.

**4. subside**    [səb'saɪd] *v*. to become weaker, less violent or less severe

At some point over the next few days or weeks the situation in Libya will calm down and oil prices will **subside**.

*Word Families*: **subsidence** *n*.

**5. homicide**    ['hɑmɪ‚saɪd] *n*. the crime of killing someone

The New York police are investigating the **homicide** of an old woman.

*Word Families*: **homicidal** *adj*

**6. ABJECT**    ['æb‚dʒekt] *adj.* miserable; wretched    **rhyming sound –ect**

From the **abject** condition of being a savage, man has risen to command the earth.

*Word Families*: **abjectly** *n*.

**7. affect**    [ə'fekt] *v*. to change or influence something; to put on a show of

The finance minister said the downturn would **affect** government finances and lead to a "temporary budget deficit".

*Word Families*: **affectation** *n*.

**8. defect**    [dɪ'fekt] *n*. a fault in someone or something; *v*. to leave a country

The exact ramification of this **defect** in the product are difficult to predict.

**9. neglect**    [nə'glekt] *v*. to fail to take care of someone; n. the failure to take care of

The woman denied that she had **neglected** her three-year old daughter.

*Word Families*: **neglectful** *adj*

**10. prospect**    [prə'spekt] *n*. the possibility that something will happen; a possible customer; *v*. to search for gold or some valuable substance

Will that **prospect** be enough to galvanize a serious response to the long-term economic problems in the United States?

# SENTENCE COMPLETION

Choose one of the new words to complete each sentence below. Make changes if necessary.

| abide | collide | confide | subside | homicide |
|-------|---------|---------|---------|----------|
| abject | affect | defect | neglect | prospect |

1. As a cold case _____ investigator, I noticed this particular crime scene.

2. The _____ of war loomed large in everyone's mind.

3. Despite his _____ by historian, Jack's views seem to have had great influence in his day.

4. Tom said he would _____ by any Commission decision on the legality of the legislation.

5. Violence has _____ after two weeks of riots.

6. One way or another, the US is finally going to _____ with fiscal reality

7. The students adored their English teacher and _____ in her.

8. The drug dealer tried to _____ to the United States but was captured by the police.

9. In India, real wage growth has lifted millions of people out of _____ poverty.

10. Arthritis is a crippling disease which _____ people all over the world

# DEFINITION MATCHING

Choose one of the new words to match each definition below.

| abide | collide | confide | subside | homicide |
|-------|---------|---------|---------|----------|
| abject | affect | defect | neglect | prospect |

11. to crash into each other        _____

12. to fail to take care of someone        _____

13. to tell someone a secret        _____

14. the possibility that something will happen     _____

15. to change or influence something     _____

16. miserable; wretched     _____

17. to become weaker, less violent or less severe     _____

18. the crime of killing someone     _____

19. to remain; to put up with     _____

20. a fault in someone or something     _____

# WRITING SENTENCES

Use each new word in the box to write an original sentence.

| abide | collide | confide | subside | homicide |
|-------|---------|---------|---------|----------|
| abject | affect | defect | neglect | prospect |

21._____

22._____

23._____

24._____

25._____

26._____

27._____

28._____

29._____

30._____

# UNIT 4

## MEMORY TIPS:

Word building with Roots, Prefixes, and Suffixes:

---

| | |
|---|---|
| **a, ab** | from, away; as *abjure, abominate* |
| **ac** | to; as *accelerate, accumulate* |
| **con** | act of; as *conjure* |
| **ob** | against; as *obscure* |

---

## NEW WORDS

| abjure | conjure | endure | obscure | immature |
|---|---|---|---|---|
| abominate | accelerate | accumulate | excoriate | matriculate |

**1. ABJURE**  [æb'dʒʊr] *v.* to give up (rights); to renounce  **rhyming sound -ure**

The conqueror tried to make the natives **abjure** their religion.

*Word Families:* **abjuration** *n.*; **abjurer** *n.*

**2. conjure**  ['kʌndʒər] *v.* to call upon supernatural forces; to appeal strongly to

No one can simply **conjure** up the money out of thin air.

*Word Families:* **conjurer** *n.*

**3. endure**  [ɪn'dʊr] *v.* to bear; to undergo hardship or strain without yielding

In the last quarter of 2012, the company **endured** heavy financial losses.

*Word Families*: **endurable** *adj.*; **endurability** *n.*; **endurably** *adv.*

**4. obscure**  [əbˈskjʊr] *adj.* unclear or abstruse; indistinct, vague; *v.* to make unclear

Some **obscure** disease has taken the fire out of her figure.

*Word Families*: **obscuration** *n.*; **obscurely** *adv.*; **obscurity** *n.*

**5. immature**  [ˌɪməˈtʃʊr] *adj.* .not fully grown or developed

God, we are so innocent and **immature** compared to this beautiful girl.

*Word Families*: **immaturity** *adj.*; **immatureness** *n.*; **immaturely** *adv*

**6. ABOMINATE** [əˈbɑmɪˌneɪt] *v.* to detest; to dislike strongly    **rhyming sound – ate**

It is a great pity that I **abominate** the slow life in the countryside.

**7. accelerate**  [əkˈseləˌreɪt] *v.* to go or cause to go faster; to speed up

The have decided to **accelerate** their research in atomic power generation and speed up the building of atomic power plants.

*Word Families*: **accelerator** *n*; **accelerable** *adj.*; **accelerative adj.**.

**8. accumulate**  [əˈkjumjəˌleɪt] *v.* to gather together in increasing quantity

However, as evidence began to **accumulate**, experts felt obliged to investigate.

*Word Families*: **accumulation** *n.*; **accumulative** *adj.*; **accumulatively** *adv.*

**9. excoriate**  [ɪkˈskɔːriːˌeɪt] *v.* to censure severely, to denounce; to scold

Whenever I did anything wrong in the office, she would proceed to **excoriate** me right in front of my fellow workers.

*Word Families*: **excoriation** *n.*

**10. matriculate**  [məˈtrɪkjəˌleɪt] *v.* to officially become a student at a university

If I want to get a law degree from Yale University, I have to **matriculate** this fall.


# SENTENCE COMPLETION

Choose one of the new words to complete each sentence below. Make changes if necessary.

| abjure | conjure | endure | obscure | immature |
|--------|---------|--------|---------|----------|
| abominate | accelerate | accumulate | excoriate | matriculate |

1. For my part, I _____ all honorable respectable toils, trials, and tribulations of every kind.

2. The new university will _____ its first students in the fall of 2018.

3. If inflation began to _____, the President said he would worry.

4. When the governor was involved in a scandal, the reporters rushed to _____ him.

5. How much longer the country can _____ foreign assets to absorb inflows is questionable.

6. The old man would enjoin the people to do the good and to _____ for committing wrong.

7. His mother, confounded by her _____ but overly and irreverent son, finally gave him up..

8. The statement the mayor made at the meeting was absolutely _____ .

9. The magician practicing witchcraft claimed that he could _____ up the spirits of the dead.

10. I cannot _____ listening to his nonsense any longer.

# DEFINITION MATCHING

Choose one of the new words to match each definition below.

| abjure | conjure | endure | obscure | immature |
|--------|---------|--------|---------|----------|
| abominate | accelerate | accumulate | excoriate | matriculate |

11. to gather together in increasing quantity _____

12. not fully grown or developed _____

13. to officially become a student at a university     _____

14. to detest; to dislike strongly     _____

15. unclear or abstruse; indistinct, vague     _____

16. to go or cause to go faster; to speed up     _____

17. to censure severely, to denounce; to scold     _____

18. to undergo hardship or strain without yielding     _____

19. to call upon supernatural forces     _____

20. to give up (rights); to renounce     _____

# WRITING SENTENCES

Use each new word in the box to write an original sentence.

| abjure | conjure | endure | obscure | immature |
|--------|---------|--------|---------|----------|
| abominate | accelerate | accumulate | excoriate | matriculate |

21._____

22._____

23._____

24._____

25._____

26._____

27._____

28._____

29._____

30._____

# UNIT 5

## MEMORY TIPS:

Word building with Roots, Prefixes, and Suffixes:

| | |
|---|---|
| **a, ab** | from, away; as *abstain, abstruse* |
| **con** | act of; as *constrain* |
| **de** | down, away from, about; as *detrain* |
| **re** | back, again; as *refrain, recluse* |

## NEW WORDS

| | | | | |
|---|---|---|---|---|
| abstain | constrain | detain | domain | refrain |
| abstruse | diffuse | effuse | profuse | recluse |

**1. ABSTAIN**    [əb'steɪn] *v.* to choose not to do something    **rhyming sound -ain**

Her family doctor asked her to **abstain** from drinking and smoking.

**2. constrain**    [kən'streɪn] *v.* to limit someone's freedom to do whatever he wants

Women are too often **constrained** by their family commitments.

*Word Families*: **constraint** *n.*; **constrainedly** *adj.*

**3. detain**    [dɪ'teɪn] *v.* to keep someone in a police station or hospital; to delay someone

The law usually allows the police to **detain** a suspect for up to 48 hours in the United States.

*Word Families*: **detainment** *n.*

**4. domain**    [doʊˈmeɪn] *n.* a particular area of activity or life;  a domain name

The Arctic remains the **domain** of the polar bear.

**5. refrain**    [rɪˈfreɪn] *v.* to stop yourself from doing something; *n.* a group of lines in a poem or a song that are repeated regularly

If you **refrain** from smoking, your health will be much better.

**6. ABSTRUSE**    [æbˈstrus] *adj.* not easy to understand   **rhyming sound – use**

Her speech was a little bit too **abstruse** for common people to understand.

*Word Families*: **abstrusely** *adj.*; **abstruseness** *n.*

**7. diffuse**    [dɪˈfjuːs] *v.* to spread over a wide area; *adj.* existing over a large area or in many areas

Over time, the technology is **diffused** and adopted by other countries.

**8. effuse**    [ɪˈfjus] *v.* to pour out words or ideas; to flow or spill out

The small town in the hidden valley **effuses** warmth and hospitality.

*Word Families*: **effusion** *n.*

**9. profuse**    [prəˈfjus] *adj.* existing or produced in large amounts

The critics were **profuse** in their praises of the new novel by the teen author.

*Word Families*: **profusion** *n*

**10. recluse**    [ˈrekˌlus] *n.* one who lives in solitude

The strange old **recluse** secluded himself from the outside world.

# SENTENCE COMPLETION

Choose one of the new words to complete each sentence below. Make changes if necessary.

| abstain | constrain | detain | domain | refrain |
|---------|-----------|--------|--------|---------|

28

| abstruse | diffuse | effuse | profuse | recluse |
|----------|---------|--------|---------|---------|

1. Japan has released the trawler and the 14 crew, but continues to _____ the ship's captain.

2. In this age of AIDS, it is absolutely necessary to _____ from unprotected sex.

3. This crisis raises fundamental questions about globalization, which was supposed to help _____ risk

4. The professor tried to _____ himself from a cough during the lecture.

5. When the police officer recognized Jennifer, he broke into _____ apologies.

6. He said that he was explaining some _____ philosophy. But to me he was only trying to stir up a storm in a teacup and mystifying things.

7. Clare's life at the dairy had been that of a _____ in respect to the world of his own class

8. Trademark law involving _____ laws is much clearer and much easier to understand, he said.

9. We should all learn to be modest and never _____ too much pride in front of others.

10. The doctor recommend that Tom _____ from consuming alcohol after his treatment.

# DEFINITION MATCHING

Choose one of the new words to match each definition below.

| abstain | constrain | detain | domain | refrain |
|---------|-----------|--------|--------|---------|
| abstruse | diffuse | effuse | profuse | recluse |

11. to spread over a wide area _____

12. to stop yourself from doing something _____

13. to keep someone in a police station or hospital _____

14. not easy to understand      _____

15. to limit someone's freedom to do something      _____

16. to pour out words or ideas      _____

17. one who lives in solitude      _____

18. to choose not to do something      _____

19. existing or produced in large amounts      _____

20. a particular area of activity or life      _____

## WRITING SENTENCES

Use each new word in the box to write an original sentence.

| abstain | constrain | detain | domain | refrain |
|---------|-----------|--------|--------|---------|
| abstruse | diffuse | effuse | profuse | recluse |

21._____

22._____

23._____

24._____

25._____

26._____

27._____

28._____

29._____

30._____

# UNIT 6

## MEMORY TIPS:

Word building with Roots, Prefixes, and Suffixes:

---

| | |
|---|---|
| **ac** | to; as accentuate, *accolade* |
| **ad** | to; as *adumbrate* |
| **co** | together; as *correlate* |
| **cent** | hundred; as *centigrade* |

---

## NEW WORDS

| accentuate | adumbrate | allocate | correlate | escalate |
|---|---|---|---|---|
| accolade | centigrade | escapade | promenade | serenade |

**1. ACCENTUATE** [æk'sentʃu,eɪt] *v.* to give force to; to stress    **rhyming sound -ate**

If the patient is suffering from shock, this drug may **accentuate** the underlying disorder.

*Word Families*: **accentuation** *n.*

**2. adumbrate**    [ə'dʌm,breɪt] *v.* to outline; to give a faint indication; to foreshadow

The recent internet development **adumbrates** a new revolution in computer science.

**3. allocate**    ['ælə,keɪt] *v.* to assign or allot for a particular purpose

The city government has **allocated** funds to build another twenty-five public schools in the next few years.

*Word Families*: **allocation** *n.*; **allocatable** *adj*

**4. correlate**   ['kɔrə,leɪt] *v.* to place in a mutual relationship; to establish a correlation

The lawyer tried every means to **correlate** the testimony of the two witnesses in the court yesterday.

*Word Families*: **correlation n.; correlative** *adj;* **correlatable** *adj.*

**5. escalate**   ['eskə,leɪt] *v.* to become worse or more serious; to increase too fast to cause a problem

The students' protest against college tuition increase **escalated** almost into a riot on Sunday.

*Word Families*: **escalation** *n.*

**6. ACCOLADE** ['ækə,leɪd] *n.* honor; award; approval   **rhyming sound – ade**

Her novel has received **accolade** from readers and critics around the world.

**7. centigrade**   ['sentɪ,greɪd] *n.* Celsius

The water in this mountain lake is minus 1.7 degrees **centigrade**, or 29 degrees Fahrenheit.

**8. escapade**   ['eskə,peɪd] *n.* something exciting or dangerous that someone is involved in

Michael said that his **escapade** was totally his own idea and it had nothing to do with his friends.

**9. promenade**   [,prɑmə'neɪd] *n.*  a walk of pleasure in a public place; v. to walk

People usually come to Jericho Beach to **promenade** on the weekend.

**10. serenade**   ['serə,neɪd] *n.* a song performed by a man outside the house of a woman he loves

The sound came over her senses and her heart as the **serenade** gives her such wonderful feeling of sweet love.


# SENTENCE COMPLETION

Choose one of the new words to complete each sentence below. Make changes if necessary.

| accentuate | adumbrate | allocate | correlate | escalate |
|---|---|---|---|---|
| accolade | centigrade | escapade | promenade | serenade |

1. Given today's world situation, even the slightest confrontation can _____ into a major war.

2. What she needs right now is nothing but the sweet music to _____ her soul.

3. Some say this street was designed as a _____ but its two sides have developed quite separately

4. In today's world situation, it is always more important to eliminate the negative than to _____ the positive.

5. We know every detail of his recent _____ in Thailand and the South Korea.

6. To be chosen to represent one's country to participate in the Olympic Games is the highest _____ for an athlete.

7. Generally speaking, research results in natural sciences rarely seem to _____ to those in arts.

8. Jenny Jones _____ that she didn't like new fashion in Hollywood.

9. The boiling point of water is 100 degrees _____.

10. The Board of Directors had a meeting to discuss how much money our company should _____ to hedge funds this year.

# DEFINITION MATCHING

Choose one of the new words to match each definition below.

| accentuate | adumbrate | allocate | correlate | escalate |
|---|---|---|---|---|
| accolade | centigrade | escapade | promenade | serenade |

11. to place in a mutual relationship _____

12. to sing a song or perform a piece of music for love _____

13. a walk of pleasure in a public place _____

14. to give a faint indication _____

15. Celsius _____

16. to assign or allot for a particular purpose _____

17. something exciting that one is involved in _____

18. to give force to; to stress _____

19. honor; award; approval _____

20. to become worse or more serious _____

# WRITING SENTENCES

Use each new word in the box to write an original sentence.

| accentuate | adumbrate | allocate | correlate | escalate |
|---|---|---|---|---|
| accolade | centigrade | escapade | promenade | serenade |

21. _____

22. _____

23. _____

24. _____

25. _____

26. _____

27. _____

28. _____

29. _____

30. _____

# UNIT 7

## MEMORY TIPS:

Word building with Roots, Prefixes, and Suffixes:

---

| | |
|---|---|
| **ac** | to; as *acquiesce,* |
| **de** | down, away, from; as *deliquesce* |
| **co** | together; as *confederate* |
| **in** | into, in, on; as *incorporate* |
| **sub** | under; as *substantiate* |

---

## NEW WORDS

| acquiesce | deliquesce | effervesce | evanesce | obsolesce |
|---|---|---|---|---|
| amalgamate | confederate | incorporate | manipulate | substantiate |

**1. ACQUIESCE** [ˌækwiˈes] *v.* to agree to do what someone wants    **rhyming sound –esce**

Jennifer's parents will never **acquiesce** in her decision to marry an old American businessman.

*Word Families*: **acquiescence** *n.*; **acquiescent** *adj.*

**2. deliquesce**    [ˌdɛlɪˈkwɛs] *v.* to dissolve gradually by absorbing moisture from the air

The fungi eventually **deliquesced**.

**3. effervesce**    [ˌɛfɚˈvɛs] *v.* to give off gas in tiny bubbles; to behave in a lively way

Harrison Hot Spring **effervesces** with bubbles all the year round.

*Word Families*: **effervescence** n.; **effervescent** *adj.*

**4. evanesce**  [ˌɛvəˈnɛs] *v.* to grow less until completely gone

I don't want the memory of our best times to **evanesce**.

*Word Families*: **evanescence** n.; **evanescent** *adj.*

**5. obsolesce**  [ˌɑbsəˈlɛs] *v.* to become obsolete

This word has not **obsolesced**, although it is rarely used.

*Word Families*: **obsolescence** n; **obsolescent** *adj.*

**6. AMALGAMATE** [əˈmælɡəˌmeɪt] *v.* to combine; to merge; to mix   **rhyming sound – ate**

The computer companies in Boulder have **amalgamated** into an international conglomerate.

**7. confederate**  [kənˈfed(ə)rət] *n.* a member of a confederacy; *adj.* united; *v.* to unite in a confederacy

The **Confederate** States perceive that they cannot carry all before them with a rush.

*Word Families*: **confederacy** n.; **confederation** n.

**8. incorporate**  [ɪnˈkɔrpəˌreɪt] *v.* to form a corporation or company; *v.* to combine

They have promised to **incorporate** environment considerations into all their policies.

**9. manipulate**  [məˈnɪpjəˌleɪt] *v.* to skillfully handle or control; to influence someone

He is a very mean person and he likes to **manipulate** people.

**10. substantiate**  [səbˈstænʃiˌeɪt] *v.* to provide evidence that proves something

He has little evidence to **substantiate** his claim that the deserted mansion belongs to his great grandparents.

# SENTENCE COMPLETION

Choose one of the new words to complete each sentence below. Make changes if necessary.

| acquiesce | deliquesce | effervesce | evanesce | obsolesce |
|-----------|------------|------------|----------|-----------|
| amalgamate | confederate | incorporate | manipulate | substantiate |

1.  The corrupted official was arrested for _____ his company's overseas financial records.

2.  The mysterious lake which is _____ with bubbles has attracted a lot of tourists recently.

3.  Nine States seceded from the Union government and established their own _____ government.

4.  When his mother asked him to stay at home to take care of the family farm, Tom willingly _____.

5.  Loan words in the English language has become _____ in modern writings.

6.  At this point the police have nothing to _____ the report

7.  Partners can decide how much they want to _____ into their own applications.

8.  This type of salt _____ very easily.

9.  The image _____ so quickly that I had no idea what it implied.

10. The School Board has decided to _____ Stony Creek School with a larger one.

# DEFINITION MATCHING

Choose one of the new words to match each definition below.

| acquiesce | deliquesce | effervesce | evanesce | obsolesce |
|-----------|------------|------------|----------|-----------|
| amalgamate | confederate | incorporate | manipulate | substantiate |

11. to become obsolete _____

12. a member of a confederacy _____

13. to grow less until completely gone  _____

14. to form a corporation  _____

15. to dissolve by absorbing moisture from the air  _____

16. to skillfully handle or control  _____

17. to provide evidence that proves something  _____

18. to agree to do what someone wants  _____

19. to merge; to combine; to mix  _____

20. to give off gas in tiny bubbles  _____

## WRITING SENTENCES

Use each new word in the box to write an original sentence.

| acquiesce | deliquesce | effervesce | evanesce | obsolesce |
|-----------|------------|------------|----------|-----------|
| amalgamate | confederate | incorporate | manipulate | substantiate |

21._____

22._____

23._____

24._____

25._____

26._____

27._____

28._____

29._____

30._____

# UNIT 8

## MEMORY TIPS:

Word building with Roots, Prefixes, and Suffixes:

---

| de | down, away, from; as *degenerate* |
|----|-----------------------------------|
| **co** | together; as *conglomerate* |
| **solv** | loosen; as *solvent* |

---

## NEW WORDS

| ambivalent | pungent | solvent | indigent | prevalent |
|------------|---------|---------|----------|-----------|
| ameliorate | conglomerate | degenerate | intoxicate | retaliate |

1.  **AMBIVALENT** [æmˈbɪvələnt] *adj.* feeling two conflicting emotions about someone or something at the same time **rhyming sound –ent**

    Jennifer remained **ambivalent** about her marriage to the billionaire.

    *Word Families*: **ambivalence** *n.*; **ambivalently** *adv.*

2. **pungent**  [ˈpʌndʒənt] *v.* having a strong sharp bitter flavor

    The more spices you use when you cook, the more **pungent** the dishes will be.

3. **solvent**  [ˈsɑlvənt] *adj.* having enough money to pay one's debts; *n.* liquid capable of dissolving other substances

When I was at college, I had to live a simple life in order to remain **solvent**.

**4. indigent** ['ɪndɪdʒənt] *adj.* very poor

The government should always bear the responsibility of taking care of the **indigent** people.

**5. prevalent** ['prevələnt] *adj.* very common in a particular place or among a particular group

The **prevalent** view is that the housing prices in Vancouver will fall in the next few months.

**6. AMELIORATE** [ə'miliə,reɪt] *v.* to improve something    **rhyming sound –ate**

The company is taking dramatic measure to **ameliorate** the working conditions of the employees.

*Word Families*: **amelioration** *n.;* **ameliorator** *n.;* **ameliorative** *adj.*

**7. conglomerate** [kən'glɑmərət] *n.* a large corporation made up of many different businesses; something made up of different things

The **conglomerate** is trying to diversify its business in the Asia-Pacific market.

**8. degenerate** [dɪ'dʒenə,reɪt] *adj.* a condition worse than normal or worse than before; *v.* to become worse; *n.* somebody regarded as retarded or corrupt

We should never allow our skepticism to **degenerate** into cynicism.

**9. intoxicate** [ɪn'tɑksɪ,ket] *v.* to make somebody drunk with alcohol

Mandy does not drink, even a tiny bit of wine will **intoxicate** her.

**10. retaliate** [rɪ'tæl,ieɪt] *v.* to repay an injury or wrong in kind

No organization or individual shall suppress, **retaliate** against or persecute a complainant.

# SENTENCE COMPLETION

Choose one of the new words to complete each sentence below. Make changes if necessary.

| ambivalent | pungent | solvent | indigent | prevalent |
|---|---|---|---|---|
| ameliorate | conglomerate | degenerate | intoxicate | retaliate |

1. When you don't know, it's easy to get it wrong; and to _____ against the wrong target.

2. Money sometimes _____ the best minds just as power the best hearts.

3. They have long shared their _____ feelings about moving to the countryside.

4. If we rely on these excessively, they can make our body functions _____ gradually.

5. Despite the fact that the disease is so _____, treatment is still far from satisfactory.

6. It is unbelievable that a billionaire had to sell his waterfront mansion in order to be _____.

7. Many social workers have attempted to _____t he conditions of people living in the slums.

8. The state university is responsible for assistance to the _____ students.

9. Starting a company or running a _____ takes a lot of sacrifices.

10. When the plants are ready to pollinate, the stem will heat up to release a _____ smell.

# DEFINITION MATCHING

Choose one of the new words to match each definition below.

| ambivalent | pungent | solvent | indigent | prevalent |
|---|---|---|---|---|
| ameliorate | conglomerate | degenerate | intoxicate | retaliate |

11. having a strong sharp bitter flavor _____

12. something made up of different things _____

13. to make somebody intensely excited _____

14. very poor _____

15. very common in a particular place _____

16. to repay an injury or wrong in kind _____

17. having enough money to pay one's debts _____

18. to improve something _____

19. to become worse _____

20. feeling two conflicting emotions at the same time _____

# WRITING SENTENCES

Use each new word in the box to write an original sentence.

| ambivalent | pungent | solvent | indigent | prevalent |
|------------|---------|---------|----------|-----------|
| ameliorate | conglomerate | degenerate | intoxicate | retaliate |

21. _____

22. _____

23. _____

24. _____

25. _____

26. _____

27. _____

28. _____

29. _____

30. _____

# UNIT 9

## MEMORY TIPS:

Word building with Roots, Prefixes, and Suffixes:

---

| | |
|---|---|
| **acious, cious** | having the quality of; as *audacious, capacious, loquacious, rapacious, sagacious, auspicious, vicious, judicious, malicious, officious* |
| **loqu** | speak; talk; as *loquacious* |
| **mal** | bad; as *malicious* |

---

## NEW WORDS

| audacious | capacious | loquacious | rapacious | sagacious |
|---|---|---|---|---|
| auspicious | vicious | judicious | malicious | officious |

**1. AUDACIOUS**  [ɔ'deɪʃəs] *adj.* bold; daring; intrepid  **rhyming sound –acious**

The millionaire was known for being **audacious** in his business dealings.

**2. capacious**  [kə'peɪʃəs] *adj.* large enough to contain a lot of things easily

This living-room is so **capacious** that you can hold a party for at least a hundred people.

**3. loquacious**  [loʊ'kweɪʃəs] *adj.* tending to talk a lot or too much

Since he came to the University of Rochester, Jack has become as **loquacious** as a politician.

*Word Families*: **loquacity** *n.;* **loquaciousness** *n.;* **loquaciously** *adv.*

**4. rapacious** [rə'peɪʃəs] *adj.* never satisfied until you have taken everything you can take

Hawks and other **rapacious** birds prey on variety of small animals.

*Word Families*: **rapaciousness** *n.;* **rapacity** *n.;* **rapaciously** *adv.*

**5. sagacious** [sə'geɪʃəs] *adj.* wise and able to make good and practical decisions

Whenever she was confused about what to do, Mary would always go to her **sagacious** grandfather for advice.

*Word Families*: **sage** *n.;* **sagaciously** *adv.*

**6. AUSPICIOUS** [ɔ'spɪʃəs] *adj.* showing signs of future success    **rhyming sound -icious**

Shakespeare's career as a playwright had an **auspicious** start.

*Word Families*: **auspiciousness** *n.;* **auspiciously** *adv.*

**7. vicious** ['vɪʃəs] *adj.* extremely violent; extremely unkind or unpleasant

He made some **vicious** statements about the President.

*Word Families*: **viciousness** *n.;* **viciously** *adv.*

**8. judicious** [dʒu'dɪʃəs] *adj.* showing intelligence and good judgment

We should always listen to the **judicious** opinions of the wise.

**9. malicious** [mə'lɪʃəs] *adj.* showing a strong feeling of wanting to hurt someone

When the girl discovered a **malicious** streak in him, she turned a deaf ear to whatever he said.

*Word Families*: **maliciousness** *n;* **maliciously** *adv.*

**10. officious** [ə'fɪʃəs] *adj.* interfering unnecessarily

When Joan returned from a trip to Vietnam, an **officious** young Customs Officer almost regarded her as a smuggler.

# SENTENCE COMPLETION

Choose one of the new words to complete each sentence below. Make changes if necessary.

| audacious | capacious | loquacious | rapacious | sagacious |
|-----------|-----------|------------|-----------|-----------|
| auspicious | vicious | judicious | malicious | officious |

1. Controversial websites raise a serious question: are we in a more _____ society than before?

2. His decision to give up smoking completely was _____.

3. They were absolutely tired of being ordered around in the office by the _____ manager.

4. The man ate with huge mouthfuls, enjoying himself vastly, his eyes shone and he was _____.

5. The author portrayed his father as a _____ drunkard in his new novel.

6. His dress consisted of a large high-crowned hat, a worn dark suit, a pair of _____ shoes.

7. Nick's first novel as a bestseller was an _____ beginning of his career as a writer.

8. In the end, it was not _____ politicians who killed the Company, but the greed and power of its managers and shareholders.

9. In the public eye, Michael is truly a _____ businessman who owns almost half of the city.

10. The college flower was nothing but a designing, _____, and unscrupulous girl from Maine.

# DEFINITION MATCHING

Choose one of the new words to match each definition below.

| audacious | capacious | loquacious | rapacious | sagacious |
|-----------|-----------|------------|-----------|-----------|
| auspicious | vicious | judicious | malicious | officious |

11. showing intelligence and good judgment          _____

12. never satisfied until one has taken what he wants     _____

13. interfering unnecessarily _____

14. daring; intrepid; bold _____

15. wise and able to make good decisions _____

16. extremely violent; extremely unkind _____

17. large enough to contain a lot of things easily _____

18. showing a strong feeling of wanting to hurt _____

19. showing signs of future success _____

20. tending to talk a lot or too much _____

## WRITING SENTENCES

Use each new word in the box to write an original sentence.

| audacious | capacious | loquacious | rapacious | sagacious |
| --- | --- | --- | --- | --- |
| auspicious | vicious | judicious | malicious | officious |

21. _____

22. _____

23. _____

24. _____

25. _____

26. _____

27. _____

28. _____

29. _____

30. _____

# UNIT 10

## MEMORY TIPS:

Word building with Roots, Prefixes, and Suffixes:

---

| | |
|---|---|
| **be** | over, about, excessively; as *behemoth* |
| **ous** | full of; as *boisterous, grievous, raucous, zealous, sumptuous* |
| **sum, sumpt** | take; as *sumptuous* |

---

## NEW WORDS

| behemoth | broth | moth | sloth | wroth |
|---|---|---|---|---|
| boisterous | grievous | raucous | zealous | sumptuous |

**1. BEHEMOTH** [bɪˈhimɑθ] *n.* someone or something that is very large, especially a company or corporation  **rhyming sound –acious**

The software **behemoth** thought that it would have an easy landing in the Asian market, but it was just a dream.

**2. broth** [brɔθ] *n.* soup, especially when it is thought to be good for you; a liquid used to give flavor when cooking

This hot and spicy **broth** tastes just like the one I used to have at home.

**3. moth** [mɒθ] *n.* insect like a butterfly that flies mostly at night

Being away abroad for a few months, most of the clothes in Mary's cupboard got **moth** in them.

47

**4. sloth**     [slɑθ] *n.* animal that lives in trees and moves slowly; a lazy person

As the saying goes: **sloth** is the mother of poverty.

*Word Families*: **sloths** *n. pl.;* **slothful** *adj.*

**5. wroth**     [slɑθ] *adj.* extremely angry; furious

If he say thus, It is well; thy servant shall have peace: but if he be very **wroth**, then be sure that evil is determined by him.

*Word Families*: **wrothful** *adj.*

**6. BOISTEROUS** ['bɔɪst(ə)rəs] *adj.* lively an noisy     **rhyming sound -icious**

He stared at their **boisterous**, laughing faces, and felt that they would have much to answer for on the day of judgment.

*Word Families*: **boisterousness** *n.;* **boisterously** *adv.*

**7. grievous**     ['grivəs] *adj.* extremely serious or severe

On hearing the news, she became **grievous** and began to cry.

*Word Families*: **grievousness** *n.;* **grievously** *adv.*

**8. raucous**     ['rɔkəs] *adj.* rude, noisy, and violent

The **raucous** sirens of the tugs came in from the Fraser River.

*Word Families*: **raucousness** *n.;* **raucously** *adv.*

**9. zealous**     ['zeləs] *adj.* full of energy, effort, and enthusiasm

He who is extremely **zealous**, skillful, and intelligent will eventually succeed in whatever he does.

**10. sumptuous**     ['sʌmptʃuəs] *adj.* impressive, expensive, and of high quality

At the party, all the distinguished guests were dressed up in their shiny and **sumptuous** evening clothes.


# SENTENCE COMPLETION

Choose one of the new words to complete each sentence below. Make changes if necessary.

| behemoth | broth | moth | sloth | wroth |
|---|---|---|---|---|
| boisterous | grievous | raucous | zealous | sumptuous |

1. The kids tended to gather together quietly for a while before they broke into _____ play.

2. For the past few months, Jack led a life of a complete _____.

3. Woe is me for my hurt! My wound is _____: but I said, truly this is a grief and I must bear it.

4. As we all know, Michael is the most _____ in performing his duties.

5. In my opinion, China may be a _____, but it is not a dinosaur.

6. Solutions that work in China might not work in India's _____ open society.

7. Joyce shared her homemade _____ with friends, although the flavor was far from palatable.

8. Then the earth shook and trembled, the foundations of heaven moved and shook, because he was _____

9. Those in the financial market have had a _____ feast and the administration is now asking the taxpayer to pick up a part of the tab.

10. The _____ habitat is being destroyed and it has nearly died out in this area.

# DEFINITION MATCHING

Choose one of the new words to match each definition below.

| behemoth | broth | moth | sloth | wroth |
|---|---|---|---|---|
| boisterous | grievous | raucous | zealous | sumptuous |

11. impressive, expensive, and of high quality  _____

12. a lazy person; being lazy  _____

13. lively and noisy  _____

14. soup; a liquid used to add flavor when cooking  _____

15. someone or something that is very large  _____

16. angry; furious  _____

17. full of energy, effort, and enthusiasm  _____

18. insect like a butterfly that flies mostly at night  _____

19. extremely serious or severe  _____

20. rude, noisy, and violent  _____

## WRITING SENTENCES

Use each new word in the box to write an original sentence.

| behemoth | broth | moth | sloth | wroth |
| --- | --- | --- | --- | --- |
| boisterous | grievous | raucous | zealous | sumptuous |

21. _____

22. _____

23. _____

24. _____

25. _____

26. _____

27. _____

28. _____

29. _____

30. _____

# UNIT 11

## MEMORY TIPS:

Word building with Roots, Prefixes, and Suffixes:

| | |
|---|---|
| **ag** | do, act; as *aghast* |
| **fore** | before; as *forecast* |
| **pict** | paint, show, draw; as *picturesque* |
| **st** | stand; as *statuesque* |

## NEW WORDS

| bombast | blast | aghast | forecast | iconoclast |
|---|---|---|---|---|
| burlesque | grotesque | picturesque | sculpturesque | staturesque |

**1. BOMBAST**   ['bɑmˌbæst] *n.* language that is full of long and pretentious words
**rhyming sound –ast**

There was no **bombast** or conceit in his presidential speech today.

*Word Families*: **bombastic** *adj.;* **bombastically** *adv.*

**2. blast**   [blæst] *n.* explosion; a sudden gust of air or wind; *v.* blow up; to damage

What the girl said aroused a **blast** of laughter in the bar.

*Word Families*: **blaster** *n.*

**3. aghast**   [əˈgæst] *adj.* shocked and upset

51

The thief stood **aghast** at the sudden arrival of the police.

**4. forecast**  ['fɔr,kæst] *n.* prediction; *v.* to predict (weather, events, etc.)

They **forecast** a large drop in unemployment over the next five years.

**5. iconoclast**  [aɪ'kɑnə,klæst] *n.* someone who attacks the beliefs, customs, and opinions that most people in society accept

Michael was an **iconoclast**. He was totally against the traditions and customs in his days.

*Word Families*: **iconoclastic** *adj.;* **iconoclastically** *adv.*

**6. BURLESQUE**  [bɜr'lesk] *n.* artistic works that satirize a subject by caricature; *adj.* satirical; *v.* to represent a serious subject in a silly way  **rhyming sound -esque**

The students' comic play was a **burlesque** of Shakespearean tragedy.

**7. grotesque**  [groʊ'tesk] *adj.* extremely ugly and strange; *n.* an ugly and strange person

The existence of this kind of person could only become the most **grotesque** of failures.

*Word Families*: **grotesqueness** *n.;* **grotesquely** *adv.*

**8. picturesque**  [ˌpɪktʃə'resk] *adj.* pleasant to look at (a place or view)

The girl tried every means to look **picturesque**, but only succeeded in being untidy.

**9. sculpturesque**  ['skʌlp tʃə'resk] *adj.* resembling sculpture

They were attracted by the **sculpturesque** beauty of the star's face.

**10. statuesque**  [ˌstætʃu'ɛsk] *adj.* resembling statue

The **statuesque** young athlete became the dream of the young girls when he won the gold medal at the Winter Olympic Games in Vancouver.

# SENTENCE COMPLETION

Choose one of the new words to complete each sentence below. Make changes if necessary.

| bombast | blast | aghast | forecast | iconoclast |
|---------|-------|--------|----------|------------|
| burlesque | grotesque | picturesque | sculpturesque | staturesque |

1. This new movie is a _____ or satirical imitation of the heroic manners of the Middle Ages.

2. According to the weather _____, there will be heavy snow in the few days.

3. Her boy friend is tall, _____, and handsome like a Hollywood action hero.

4. The powerful young stood against the cliff and looked _____ and determined.

5. The police were reported to have _____ their way into the drug dealer's house using explosives

6. Their early films tried to convey revolutionary propaganda through _____ and fantastic imagery.

7. Jennifer looked _____ at the extent of the damage to her car.

8. The United States missiles have _____ and descriptive names.

9. There is no _____ or chauvinism or phony sentiment in Mr. Obama's oratory.

10. Jack was rumored to be an _____ in college because he refused to be bound by traditions.

# DEFINITION MATCHING

Choose one of the new words to match each definition below.

| bombast | blast | aghast | forecast | iconoclast |
|---------|-------|--------|----------|------------|
| burlesque | grotesque | picturesque | sculpturesque | staturesque |

11. pleasant to look at (a place or view)          _____

12. resembling statue          _____

13. prediction _____

14. extremely ugly and strange _____

15. satirical; to imitate satirically _____

16. language that is full of pretentious words _____

17. person who attacks traditional beliefs and customs _____

18. resembling sculpture _____

19. explosion; to blow up _____

20. shocked and upset _____

## WRITING SENTENCES

Use each new word in the box to write an original sentence.

| bombast | blast | aghast | forecast | iconoclast |
|---------|-------|--------|----------|------------|
| burlesque | grotesque | picturesque | sculpturesque | staturesque |

21. _____

22. _____

23. _____

24. _____

25. _____

26. _____

27. _____

28. _____

29. _____

30. _____

# UNIT 12

## MEMORY TIPS:

Word building with Roots, Prefixes, and Suffixes:

---

| | |
|---|---|
| **ish** | having the character of; as *burnish, anguish, furnish, garnish, tarnish,* |
| **ang** | angular; as *anguish* |

---

## NEW WORDS

| | | | | |
|---|---|---|---|---|
| burnish | anguish | furnish | garnish | tarnish |
| burrow | billow | escrow | marrow | shallow |

**1. BURNISH**     ['bɜrnɪʃ] *v.* to rub metal until it shines; *v.* to improve your reputation
**rhyming sound –ish**

The current leadership has sought to **burnish** its image with various cleanup campaigns.

*Word Families*: **burnisher** *n.*

**2. anguish**     ['æŋgwɪʃ] *n.* extreme anxiety or torment; *v.* cause to feel anguish

With **anguish** she wished she could do something for the wretched young man.

**3. furnish**     ['fɜrnɪʃ] *v.* to provide furniture for a room or house; to provide someone with something

Many five-star hotels are **furnished** with antiques and expensive art works.

**4. garnish**    ['gɑrnɪʃ] *n.* something you add to a dish; *v.* to decorate (food)

The turkey was served with a **garnish** of parsley.

*Word Families*: **garnishment** *n.*

**5. tarnish**    ['tɑrnɪʃ] *v.* to make or become stained or less bright; *n.* discoloration or blemish

The Prime Minister said that he will help to improve the **tarnished** reputation of his country.

*Word Families*: **tarnishable** *adj.*

**6. BURROW**    ['bʌroʊ] *n.* a hole or tunnel in the ground made by an animal; *v.* to dig holes in the ground; to push your hands into or under something  **rhyming sound -ow**

To finish my term paper on time, I had to **burrow** in the library for the books I needed.

*World Families*: **burrower** *n.*

**7. billow**    ['bɪloʊ] *n.* a large wave in the ocean; to rise up or swell out

An angry **billow** almost swallowed the small fish boat.

*Word Families*: **billowy** *adj.*.

**8. escrow**    ['eskroʊ] *n.* money, property, or a legal document that is kept by someone until a particular thing has happened

The billionaire has only five million dollars in his **escrow** account for his children.

**9. marrow**    ['meroʊ] *n.* the soft substance inside bones where blood cells develop

The woman hates her lazy husband to the **marrow**.

**10. shallow**    ['ʃæloʊ] *adj.* not deep; lacking depth of character or intellect; *n.* area of shallow water

I am absolutely sure that he is **shallow**, vain, and untrustworthy.

*Word Families*: **shallowness** *n.;* **shallowly** *adv.*

# SENTENCE COMPLETION

Choose one of the new words to complete each sentence below. Make changes if necessary.

| burnish | anguish | furnish | garnish | tarnish |
|---------|---------|---------|---------|---------|
| burrow  | billow  | escrow  | marrow  | shallow |

1. I see honors, happiness, success, shining upon every _____ of the dark gulf beneath which I must sink at last.

2. The little boy waited patiently for the rabbit to come out of the _____.

3. Moisture leads to the _____ of the silverware.

4. A friend of ours closed _____ on his new home last Friday.

5. Lotus jackets could further _____ the brand, which stresses textile innovation.

6. The rent for this _____ apartment is only two thousand dollars a month.

7. Mary had her beef sandwich with some limp salad _____.

8. The very thought of the fatal car accident chilled her to _____.

9. The poor guy's _____ was so great that it turned into madness.

10. She took off her shoes and waded across the _____ creek.

# DEFINITION MATCHING

Choose one of the new words to match each definition below.

| burnish | anguish | furnish | garnish | tarnish |
|---------|---------|---------|---------|---------|
| burrow  | billow  | escrow  | marrow  | shallow |

11. discoloration or blemish _____

12. lacking depth of character and intellect _____

13. to provide someone with something _____

14. the soft substance inside bones _____

15. money kept by someone until something happens _____

16. to improve your reputation _____

17. a large ocean wave _____

18. extreme anxiety or torment _____

19. to dig a hole in the ground _____

20. to decorate (food) _____

## WRITING SENTENCES

Use each new word in the box to write an original sentence.

| burnish | anguish | furnish | garnish | tarnish |
|---------|---------|---------|---------|---------|
| burrow | billow | escrow | marrow | shallow |

21. _____

22. _____

23. _____

24. _____

25. _____

26. _____

27. _____

28. _____

29. _____

30. _____

# UNIT 13

## MEMORY TIPS:

Word building with Roots, Prefixes, and Suffixes:

---

**con**          fully; as *congeal, conceal, contentious,*

**ious**         characterized by; as *contentious, abstentious, licentious, pretentious, sententious*

**sent**         feel, think; as *sententious*

---

## NEW WORDS

| congeal | heal | appeal | conceal | ordeal |
|---------|------|--------|---------|--------|
| contentious | abstentious | licentious | pretentious | sententious |

**1. CONGEAL**  [kən'dʒil] *v.* to become thick and solid   **rhyming sound –eal**

Water can **congeal** to be ice, sweat can **congeal** to be resplendence.

*Word Families*: **congealness** *n.;* **congealable** *adj.*

**2. heal**  [hil] *v.* to make or become well

Time can help us **heal** all our sorrows.

**3. appeal**  [ə'pil] *v.* to make an urgent request; to attract or please; *n.* earnest request

The Premier **appealed** to the young people to use their votes.

*Word Families*: **appealer** *n.;* **appellant** *adj.*

**4. conceal**    [kən'sil] *v.* to hide something; to prevent someone from seeing or knowing your feelings

Mary knew at once that Michael was **concealing** something very important from her.

*Word Families*: **concealment** *n.*

**5. ordeal**    [ɔr'dil] *n.* an extremely unpleasant experience, especial one that lasts for a long time

The **ordeal** of virtue is to resist all temptation to evil.

**6. CONTENTIOUS** [kən'tenʃəs] *adj.* causing disagreement between people or groups; enjoy arguing with people   **rhyming sound -ious**

There is a **contentious** clause in the agreement, therefore, we can't sign.

*Word Families*: **contentiousness** *n.;* **contentiously** *adv.*

**7. abstentious**    [æb'stenʃəs] *adj.* self-restraining; avoid something, such as food or sex

The old man lives an **abstentious** life and he has no friends.

**8. licentious**    [laɪ'senʃəs] *adj.* very interested in sex in a way that is unpleasant or offensive

To the **licentious** person, grace becomes a cheap gift that holds very little genuine value.

*Word Families*: **licentiousness** *n.;* **licentiously** *adv.*

**9. pretentious**    [prɪ'tenʃəs] *adj.* making (unjustified) claims to special merit or importance

Helen is a talented and **pretentious** writer.

*Word Families*: **pretentiousness** *n.;* **pretentiously** *adv.*

**10. sententious**    [sen'tenʃəs] *adj.* trying to sound wise; pompously moralizing

This man likes to express himself in **sententious** phrases and quotations, spoken in low voice.

# SENTENCE COMPLETION

Choose one of the new words to complete each sentence below. Make changes if necessary.

| congeal | heal | appeal | conceal | ordeal |
|---|---|---|---|---|
| contentious | abstentious | licentious | pretentious | sententious |

1. Though great artists have been _____, license does not necessarily result in great art.

2. Usually, Big Ben's mellow voice comes clear, _____, reassuring over the air.

3. Joyce made one last _____ to her mother for permission to go to the party.

4. The Hollywood actress was neither affected nor _____.

5. We should _____ our heritage into distinct national identity.

6. Being lost on an island for five years was an _____ for the young girl.

7. The artist is a recluse and it seems that he enjoys his _____ lifestyle.

8. The psychological effects on the United States were immense and in Washington the wounds have still not fully _____.

9. She is definitely not the kind of _____ girl people usually see.

10. I promised that I will never _____ anything from you.

# DEFINITION MATCHING

Choose one of the new words to match each definition below.

| congeal | heal | appeal | conceal | ordeal |
|---|---|---|---|---|
| contentious | abstentious | licentious | pretentious | sententious |

11. making unjustified claims to something _____

12. enjoy arguing with people _____

13. to make or become well _____

14. trying to sound wise; pompously moralizing _____

15. self-restraining                         _____

16. to hide something from someone           _____

17. very interested in sex                    _____

18. to become thick and solid                _____

19. earnest request                          _____

20. an extremely unpleasant experience       _____


# WRITING SENTENCES

Use each new word in the box to write an original sentence.

| congeal | heal | appeal | conceal | ordeal |
|---------|------|--------|---------|--------|
| contentious | abstentious | licentious | pretentious | sententious |


21. _____

22. _____

23. _____

24. _____

25. _____

26. _____

27. _____

28. _____

29. _____

30. _____

# UNIT 14

## MEMORY TIPS:

Word building with Roots, Prefixes, and Suffixes:

---

| | |
|---|---|
| **con** | together**;** as *contravene, converge* |
| **ob** | against; as *obscene* |
| **se** | apart, away; as *serene* |
| **merg** | plunge, sink; as *merge, emerge, immerge, submerge* |

---

## NEW WORDS

| contravene | gene | hygiene | obscene | serene |
|---|---|---|---|---|
| converge | merge | diverge | emerge | submerge |

1. **CONTRAVENE** [ˌkɑntrəˈvin] *v.* to do something that is not allow by the law, rule or

    agreement   **rhyming sound –ene**

    They have banned the film on the grounds that it **contravenes** criminal libel laws

2. **gene**    [dʒin] *n.* part of a cell which determines the inherited characteristics

    **Gene** mutations are alterations in the DNA code.

3. **hygiene**    [ˈhaɪdʒin] *n.* principles and practice of health and cleanliness

    Everyone should be extremely careful about personal **hygiene**.

**4. obscene**     [ab'sin] *adj.* offensive in a sexual way

The judge has ruled that the novel is **obscene** and copies should be destroyed.

*Word Families*: **obscenely** *adj.*

**5. serene**     [sə'rin] *adj.* calm or peaceful

The girl didn't speak much, she just looked at me with that **serene** smile of hers.

*Word Families*: **serenely** *adj.*

**6. CONVERGE**     [kən'vɜrdʒ] *v.* to come from different direction to reach the same point
**rhyming sound -erge**

As they flow south, the five rivers **converge**.

**7. merge**     [mɜrdʒ] *v.* to combine or blend

The two companies finally **merged** to cut operating costs.

*Word Families*: **merger** *n.*

**8. diverge**     [daɪ'vɜrdʒ] *v.* to start to go in separate directions; to become different after being the same

I firmly believe that our opinions **diverge** from a common starting point.

*Word Families*: **divergence** *n*

**9. emerge**     [ɪ'mɜrdʒ] *v.* to come out of something or out from behind something

Man has gradually **emerged** from barbarism into civilization.

*Word Families*: **emergence** *n.;* **emergency** *n.*

**10. submerge**     [səb'mɜr(r)dʒ] *v.* to put or go below the surface of the water or other liquid

At the first sign of danger the submarine would **submerge**.

# SENTENCE COMPLETION

Choose one of the new words to complete each sentence below. Make changes if necessary.

| contravene | gene | hygiene | obscene | serene |
|---|---|---|---|---|
| converge | merge | diverge | emerge | submerge |

1. Competitors from more than a hundred countries have _____ .on Sheffield for the Games

2. She was eager to _____ herself in the feminist movement.

3. Monica received a very _____ phone call last night.

4. These issues will be difficult to deal with in Asia where country responses will _____ .

5. A known _____ with a desirable quality can be inserted into a rice plant.

6. The rivers _____ just north of a vital irrigation system

7. Their course of study includes elementary _____ and medical theory.

8. We must make sure that the content of the settlement agreement shall not _____ the law.

9. After all, you never know where the next breakthrough technology might _____ .

10. While traveling in the Rockies, I found that the life in the deep mountains was truly _____ .

# DEFINITION MATCHING

Choose one of the new words to match each definition below.

| contravene | gene | hygiene | obscene | serene |
|---|---|---|---|---|
| converge | merge | diverge | emerge | submerge |

11. to go below the surface of the water _____

12. offensive in a sexual way _____

13. to start to go in separate directions _____

14. part of a cell carrying the inherited characteristics _____

15. to become known; to come out of something        _____

16. calm and peaceful                                _____

17. to combine or blend                              _____

18. to do something not allowed by the law or rule   _____

19. to come from all directions to reach the same point_____

20. principles and practices of health and cleanliness _____

## WRITING SENTENCES

Use each new word in the box to write an original sentence.

| contravene | gene | hygiene | obscene | serene |
|------------|------|---------|---------|--------|
| converge | merge | diverge | emerge | submerge |

21._____

22._____

23._____

24._____

25._____

26._____

27._____

28._____

29._____

30._____

# UNIT 15

## MEMORY TIPS:

Word building with Roots, Prefixes, and Suffixes:

| | |
|---|---|
| **ex** | out of, from; as *expurgate, exaggerate* |
| **ious** | characterized by; as *copious, dubious, obvious, previous, mischievous* |
| **pro** | forward, before; as *promulgate* |

## NEW WORDS

| copious | dubious | odious | commodious | mischievous |
|---|---|---|---|---|
| corroborate | expurgate | promulgate | affiliate | exaggerate |

**1. COPIOUS**   ['koʊpiəs] *adj.* large, or in large amounts   **rhyming sound –ous**

The professor's speech was fluent, but it was also a little bit **copious**.

*Word Families*: **copiousness** *n*.; **copiously** *adv*.

**2. dubious**   ['dubiəs] *adj* .not sure about the truth or quality of something

Those figures alone are a **dubious** basis for such a conclusion.

**3. odious**   ['oʊdiəs] *adj.* very unpleasant

This deserted temple has an **odious** smell, something must be rotten.

**4. commodious**   [kə'moʊdiəs] *adj.* very roomy, spacious

Their habitation was not merely respectable and **commodious**, but even dignified and imposing.

**5. mischievous**   ['mɪstʃɪvəs] *adj.* full of mischief; intended to cause harm

The Prime Minister's office has dismissed the story as **mischievous** and false.

*Word Families*: **mischief** *n.*; **mischievously** *adv.*

**6. CORROBORATE** [kə'rɑbə,reɪt] *v.* to support what someone says by giving information that

agrees with it   **rhyming sound -ate**

As a result, a lot of investors say, ratings in structured finance are hard to **corroborate** independently.

*Word Families*: **corroboration** *n.;* **corroborator** *n.;* **corroborative** *adj.*

**7. expurgate**   ['ɛkspɚ,get] *v.* to remove words or passages considered offensive or unsuitable from works, etc.

This book was first publish 1898 in a highly **expurgated** version.

**8. promulgate**   ['prɑməl,get, pro'mʌl,get] *v.* put (a law, etc.) into effect by announcing it officially; to make widely known

In order to regulate franchise effectively, western countries have **promulgated** special laws.

*Word Families*: **promulgation** *n.*

**9. affiliate**   [ə'fɪli,eɪt] *n.* an organization that is connected with a larger group; v. to link up with a larger group

In 2007, the bank opened its own securities **affiliate** called Sony Securities.

*Word Families*: **affiliative** *adj.*

**10. exaggerate**   [ɪg'zædʒə,ret] *v.* regard or represent as greater than is true

Say whatever your memory suggests as true, but add nothing and **exaggerate** nothing.

*Word Families*: **exaggeration** *n.;* **exaggerative** *adj.;* **exaggeratedly** *adj.*

# SENTENCE COMPLETION

Choose one of the new words to complete each sentence below. Make changes if necessary.

| copious | dubious | odious | commodious | mischievous |
|---|---|---|---|---|
| corroborate | expurgate | promulgate | affiliate | exaggerate |

1. Tommy is a _____ but lovable boy.

2. Michael always _____ to make his romantic stories more amusing.

3. The police raided the night club and arrested several _____ characters.

4. The Government will not allow the staff association to _____ with outside unions.

5. Nothing was more _____ to me than the company that was there.

6. The president's speech was fluent, but it was also _____.

7. China should _____ Law on State Immunity and make clear restrictive immunity.

8. I have just bought an _____ edition of Wordsworth's poems published in 1918.

9. As a result, many investors say, ratings in structured finance are hard to _____ independently.

10. This apartment is not _____ enough for the five of us to live in.

# DEFINITION MATCHING

Choose one of the new words to match each definition below.

| copious | dubious | odious | commodious | mischievous |
|---|---|---|---|---|
| corroborate | expurgate | promulgate | affiliate | exaggerate |

11. regard or represent as greater than is true _____

12. to link up with a larger group _____

13. very unpleasant _____

14. not sure about the truth or quality of something    _____

15. to make something (a law, etc.) widely known    _____

16. roomy, spacious    _____

17. .to support what someone says with evidence    _____

18. to remove offensive content from works, etc.    _____

19. large, or in large amounts    _____

20. full of mischief    _____

# WRITING SENTENCES

Use each new word in the box to write an original sentence.

| copious | dubious | odious | commodious | mischievous |
|---------|---------|--------|------------|-------------|
| corroborate | expurgate | promulgate | affiliate | exaggerate |

21. _____

22. _____

23. _____

24. _____

25. _____

26. _____

27. _____

28. _____

29. _____

30. _____

# UNIT 16

## MEMORY TIPS:

Word building with Roots, Prefixes, and Suffixes:

---

| | |
|---|---|
| **able** | able; as *culpable, blamable, censurable, reproachable, unbearable* |
| **ory** | a place for; as *cursory, mandatory, promissory, conservatory, observatory* |
| **re** | back, again; as *reproachable* |
| **un** | not; as *unbearable* |

---

## NEW WORDS

| culpable | blamable | censurable | reproachable | unbearable |
|---|---|---|---|---|
| cursory | mandatory | promissory | conservatory | observatory |

**1. CULPABLE**   ['kʌlpəb(ə)l] *adj.* responsible for doing something bad or illegal   **rhyming sound –able**

The director's decision to do nothing makes him absolutely **culpable**.

*Word Families*: **culpability** *n.;* **culpably** *adv.*

**2. blamable**   ['bleməbəl] *adj.* consider someone responsible for something

An exaggeration is a blood relation to falsehood and nearly as **blamable**.

*Word Families*: **blame** *n.*

**3. censurable**   ['sɛnʃərəbəl] *adj.* deserving blame or criticism

71

The president of the company is to blame for his **censurable** misconduct.

*Word Families*: **censure** *n.*

**4. reproachable**     [riˈprəutʃəbl] *adj.* deserving rebuke or blame

We believe that too great subtleness in law is definitely **reproachable**.

*Word Families*: **reproach** *n.*

**5. unbearable**     [ʌnˈbɛrəbəl] *adj.* not able to be endured; extremely painful

At the thought of his poor mother, an **unbearable** sense of shame possessed the man.

*Word Families*: **unbearableness** *n.;* **unbearably** *adv.*

**6. CURSORY**     [ˈkɜrsəri] *adj.* quick and not thorough     **rhyming sound -ory**

A **cursory** inspection of the house failed to reveal its structural flaws.

*Word Families*: **cursoriness** *n.;* **cursorily** *adv.*

**7. mandatory**     [ˈmændəˌtɔri, -ˌtori] *adj.* ordered by law or rule; compulsory

The officers will undergo **mandatory** counseling during their administrative leave.

*Word Families*: **mandate** *n.;* **mandatorily** *adv.*

**8. promissory**     [ˈprɑmɪˌsɔri, -ˌsori] *adj.* concerning, containing, or implying a promise

A bond is a **promissory** note, usually issued for a specified amount.

**9. conservatory**     [kənˈsɜrvəˌtɔri] *n.* a room with glass wall and glass roof, attached to a house; school where students study to become professional musicians or actors

New York **Conservatory** of Music is one of the best in the world.

*Word Families*: **conservatories** *n. pl.*

**10. observatory**     [əbˈzɜrvəˌtɔri] *n.* building equipped for studying the weather and stars.

Officials from Greenwich **Observatory** have the clock checked twice a day.

# SENTENCE COMPLETION

Choose one of the new words to complete each sentence below. Make changes if necessary.

| culpable | blamable | censurable | reproachable | unbearable |
|----------|----------|------------|--------------|------------|
| cursory | mandatory | promissory | conservatory | observatory |

1. When you borrow money from a bank, you have to signs a _____ note.

2. Jordon was fired on the spot because of his _____ conduct in the office.

3. Some books are for intensive study and some are for _____ reading.

4. When Bill built the mansion, he wanted the _____ to be integrated with the kitchen.

5. Peach town is a place of _____ dullness, conformity, hypocrisy, and oppression.

6. There is no doubt that the mayor is _____ for the shortage of electricity in the small town.

7. Attendance at the fund-raising meeting on Friday is _____ for all the students.

8. I can't be held _____ for other people's mistakes in this matter.

9. The local _____ has just alerted the residents that there would be a snow storm tomorrow.

10. I believe that Jack is definitely _____ for the company's loss of revenue this month.

# DEFINITION MATCHING

Choose one of the new words to match each definition below.

| culpable | blamable | censurable | reproachable | unbearable |
|----------|----------|------------|--------------|------------|
| cursory | mandatory | promissory | conservatory | observatory |

11. building equipped for weather and stars study   _____

12. deserving rebuke or blame   _____

13. school for professional musicians or actors _____

14. responsible for doing something bad or illegal _____

15. concerning, containing or implying a promise _____

16. consider someone responsible for _____

17. quick and not thorough _____

18. deserving blame or criticism _____

19. compulsory _____

20. not able to be endured _____

## WRITING SENTENCES

Use each new word in the box to write an original sentence.

| culpable | blamable | censurable | reproachable | unbearable |
|---|---|---|---|---|
| cursory | mandatory | promissory | conservatory | observatory |

21._____

22._____

23._____

24._____

25._____

26._____

27._____

28._____

29._____

30._____

# UNIT 17

## MEMORY TIPS:

Word building with Roots, Prefixes, and Suffixes:

---

| | |
|---|---|
| **con** | together; as *concrete* |
| **de** | down, away from, about; as *deplete* |
| **dis** | apart, not; as *discrete, discrepancy* |
| **ob** | against; as *obsolete* |

---

## NEW WORDS

| deplete | concrete | discrete | replete | obsolete |
|---|---|---|---|---|
| discrepancy | chancy | fancy | necromancy | sycophancy |

**1. DEPLETE**  [dɪ'plit] *v.* to reduce the amount of something or the number of things
**rhyming sound –ete**

Most native animal species have been severely **depleted** because of the deforestation on this island.

*Word Families*: **depletion** *n.*

**2. concrete**  ['kɑŋˌkrit] *n.* mixture of cement, sand, stone, and water, used in building; *adj.*

made of concrete, based on facts and information

They had no **concrete** evidence against Michael for bribery.

*Word Families*: **concreteness** *n.;* **concretely** *adv.*

**3. discrete** [dɪ'skrit] *adj.* separate

The computer giant is made up of many small, **discrete** units.

*Word Families*: **discreteness** *n.;* **discretely** *adv.*

**4. replete** [rɪ'plit] *adj.* full of something

Everyone is dreaming of a home **replete** with warmth and comfort.

*Word Families*: **repletion** *n.*

**5. obsolete** [ˌɑbsə'lit] *adj.* no longer used because of being outdated

These computers are **obsolete** and nobody wants to buy them.

*Word Families*: **obsoleteness** *n.;* **obsoletism** *n.* **obsoletely** *adv.*

**6. DISCREPANCY** [dɪ'skrepənsi] *n.* a difference between things that should be the same

**rhyming sound -ancy**

There was a **discrepancy** in the two reports about the car accident.

*Word Families*: **discrepant** *adj.*

**7. chancy** ['tʃænsi] *adj.* uncertain, risky

That was a **chancy** thing to do ; you could have been badly injured

**8. fancy** ['fænsi] *adj.* elaborate, not plain; *n.* sudden irrational liking or desire; imagination; *v.* to believe that something is true.

She **fancied** that Tom would buy her a new BMW for her birthday.

**9. necromancy** ['nekrəˌmænsi] *n.* communication with the dead; sorcery

Fielding was not ashamed to practice a little **necromancy**.

*Word Families*: **necromancer** *n;* **necromantic** *adj.*

**10. sycophancy** ['sɪkəfənsi] *n.* flattery

The problem with **sycophancy** isn't so much that it's offensive to watch, but that it's a lousy business strategy.

## SENTENCE COMPLETION

Choose one of the new words to complete each sentence below. Make changes if necessary.

| deplete | concrete | discrete | replete | obsolete |
|---------|----------|----------|---------|----------|
| discrepancy | chancy | fancy | necromancy | sycophancy |

1. _____ is the kind of human weakness I can never tolerate.

2. We must break away with the_____ rules and regulations.

3. The magic of _____ is nothing but deceiving people.

4. We must try our best not to _____ the earth of its natural resources.

5. His last look was a bold and, in a way, surrealistic mixture of fact and _____.

6. Her story about her overseas travels was _____ with falsehood.

7. The army general never came up with a _____ proposal to end the civil war.

8. So far the _____ in the annual report has not been satisfactorily explained.

9. The university is composed of _____ heavenly bodies.

10. If this method of progress seems _____ and wasteful, it has the merit of its faults.

## DEFINITION MATCHING

Choose one of the new words to match each definition below.

| deplete | concrete | discrete | replete | obsolete |
|---------|----------|----------|---------|----------|
| discrepancy | chancy | fancy | necromancy | sycophancy |

11. flattery                              _____

12. communication with the dead           _____

13. to reduce the amount of something     _____

14. uncertain, risky _____

15. elaborate, not plain _____

16. based on facts and information _____

17. full of something _____

18. a difference between things that are the same _____

19. separate _____

20. no longer used because of being outdated _____

# WRITING SENTENCES

Use each new word in the box to write an original sentence.

| deplete | concrete | discrete | replete | obsolete |
|---------|----------|----------|---------|----------|
| discrepancy | chancy | fancy | necromancy | sycophancy |

21._____

22._____

23._____

24._____

25._____

26._____

27._____

28._____

29._____

30._____

# UNIT 18

## MEMORY TIPS:

Word building with Roots, Prefixes, and Suffixes:

---

| | |
|---|---|
| **aer, aero** | air, atmosphere, aviation; as *aerospace* |
| **con** | together**;** as *conflate* |
| **dis** | apart, not; as *disgrace* |
| **inter** | between, among; as *interface* |

---

## NEW WORDS

| | | | | |
|---|---|---|---|---|
| efface | disgrace | retrace | aerospace | interface |
| elucidate | abate | conflate | rebate | stagnate |

**1. EFFACE**  [ɪˈfeɪs] *v.* to make something disappear; to remove a memory or feeling from someone's mind   **rhyming sound –ace**

Time alone will **efface** the unpleasant memories in our lives.

*Word Families*: **effacement** *n.*; **effaceable** *adj.*

**2. disgrace**  [dɪsˈgreɪs] *n.* the loss of other people's respect; *v.* to harm the reputation of a person or group

The president had to resign in **disgrace** because of the scandal.

**3. retrace** [ˌriˈtreɪs] *v.* to go back over ( route, etc.) again; to discover where someone or something has been by examining evidence

Women usually **retrace** their steps before selecting the clothes they want to try on.

**4. aerospace** [ˈeroʊˌspeɪs] *n.* the atmosphere of the earth and the space beyond it; *adj.* relating to the science of building airplanes and space vehicles.

Now all four companies have merged into **aerospace** titan – Boeing.

**5. interface** [ˈɪntərˌfeɪs] *n.* area where two things interact or link; circuit linking a computer and another device

The client code can assume an **interface** will never change.

**6. ELUCIDATE** [ɪˈlusɪˌdeɪt] *v.* to make something easier to understand by giving more information     **rhyming sound -ate**

Her true purpose was not to **elucidate** but to addle at the meeting.

*Word Families*: **elucidation** *n.;* **elucidator** *n.;* **elucidatory** *adj.*

**7. abate** [əˈbeɪt] *v.* to become less serious or extreme gradually

The doctor gave her some medicine to **abate** the pain.

**8. conflate** [kənˈfleɪt] *v.* to combine two or more things

When we talk about financial matters, people often make mistakes by **conflating** money with wealth.

*Word Families*: **conflation** *n.*

**9. rebate** [ˈriˌbeɪt] *n.* discount or refund

Residents in Richmond are entitled to a **rebate** on their electricity bills this year.

**10. stagnate** [ˈstæɡˌneɪt] *adj.* to stay the same without growing or developing

The nation's economy is likely to **stagnate** for a long time to come.

# SENTENCE COMPLETION

Choose one of the new words to complete each sentence below. Make changes if necessary.

| efface | disgrace | retrace | aerospace | interface |
|--------|----------|---------|-----------|-----------|
| elucidate | abate | conflate | rebate | stagnate |

1. My computer has a network _____, which allows me to get to other computers.

2. We should try our best to _____ the noise pollution in our cities.

3. Does the ability to map the unknown deserve less credit from society than the ability to _____ the known?

4. Generally speaking, women don't like to obtain positions of power because they tend to _____ themselves.

5. Professor Peck used aphid fecundity data to _____ the theoretical effects of antibiosis on insect population dynamics.

6. It would be a mistake to _____ the rise of China with the rise of Asia.

7. Judy is an _____ engineer, and works for Orlando Aircraft Corporation.

8. It goes against our principle to give _____ to our clients.

9. The strong woman would as soon die as _____ herself in front of her enemies.

10. Industry will _____ if we do not stimulate our economy.


# DEFINITION MATCHING

Choose one of the new words to match each definition below.

| efface | disgrace | retrace | aerospace | interface |
|--------|----------|---------|-----------|-----------|
| elucidate | abate | conflate | rebate | stagnate |

11. stay the same without growing or developing _____

12. to discover where someone or something has been_____

13. refund or discount _____

14. to combine two or more things. _____

15. to make something disappear _____

16. to make something easier to understand _____

17. to become less serious or extreme _____

18. relating to the science of flying airplanes _____

19. the loss of other people's respect _____

20. area where two things interact or link _____

## WRITING SENTENCES

Use each new word in the box to write an original sentence.

| efface | disgrace | retrace | aerospace | interface |
|--------|----------|---------|-----------|-----------|
| elucidate | abate | conflate | rebate | stagnate |

21._____

22._____

23._____

24._____

25._____

26._____

27._____

28._____

29._____

30._____

# UNIT 19

## MEMORY TIPS:

Word building with Roots, Prefixes, and Suffixes:

| | |
|---|---|
| **ic** | of, like; as *enigmatic, pragmatic, schematic, traumatic, charismatic* |
| **pre** | before; as *preview* |
| **over** | excessive, above; as *overview* |

## NEW WORDS

| enigmatic | phlegmatic | pragmatic | traumatic | charismatic |
|---|---|---|---|---|
| eschew | shrew | curfew | overview | purview |

**1. ENIGMATIC**    [ˌenɪɡ'mætɪk] *adj.* mysterious and difficult to understand    **rhyming sound –atic**

The beautiful actress had an **enigmatic** smile on her face.

*Word Families*: **enigmatical** *adj.*; **enigmatically** *adv.*

**2. phlegmatic**    [fleɡ'mætɪk] *adj.* able to be calm in a dangerous or frightening situation

The economist was a stubby, **phlegmatic**, shrewd person.

**3. pragmatic**    [præɡ'mætɪk] *adj.* involving or emphasizing practical results rather than theories and ideas

This was true to his **pragmatic** temperament.

**4. traumatic**    [trɔ'mætɪk] *adj.* emotionally shocked; injured or wounded

She suffered a nervous breakdown. It was a **traumatic** experience for her.

*Word Families*: **trauma** *n.;* **traumatically** *adv.*

**5. charismatic**    [ˌkerɪz'mætɪk] *adj.* having the power to influence and attract people

Traditional and **charismatic** leaders are authoritative over belief and value.

*Word Families*: **charisma** *n.*; **charismatically** *adv.*

**6. ESCHEW**    [es'tʃu] *v.* to avoid doing something, especially for moral reasons
**rhyming sound -ew**

Although he appeared to enjoy a jet-setting life, he **eschewed** publicity and avoided nightclubs.

**7. shrew**    [ʃru] *n.* a small mouselike animal; bad tempered nagging woman

Tom found that he has just married to a vulgar **shrew**.

*Word Families*: **shrewishness** *n.;* **shrewish** *adj.;* **shrewishly** *adv.*

**8. curfew**    ['kɜr,fju] *n.* law ordering people to stay inside their homes after a specific time at night; time set as deadline by such a law

The village was placed under **curfew**.

*Word Families*: **curfews** *n.pl.*

**9. overview**    ['oʊvər,vju] *n.* a description of the main features of something

The opening chapter gives a brief historical **overview** of economics.

*Word Families*: **overviews** *n.pl.*

**10. purview**    ['pɜrvju] *n.* the area of responsibility a person or organization has

These are questions that lie outside the **purview** of our inquiry.

## SENTENCE COMPLETION

Choose one of the new words to complete each sentence below. Make changes if necessary.

| enigmatic | phlegmatic | pragmatic | traumatic | charismatic |
|-----------|------------|-----------|-----------|-------------|
| eschew | shrew | curfew | overview | purview |

1. The profile of the company includes an _____ , business scope , and financial outlook.

2. She played an intermittent and somewhat _____ part in Sebastian's drama.

3. We find that attempts aimed at using the Security Council to discuss issues outside its _____ are unacceptable.

4. Whales are the most _____ of all sea creatures.

5. The American people are _____ by nature.

6. Every man can rule a _____ but he who has her.

7. A civilized leader must _____ violence.

8. The European character is often said to be _____ .

9. No one walked in the street, for the _____ was strict

10. For a child the death of a pet can be _____

# DEFINITION MATCHING

Choose one of the new words to match each definition below.

| enigmatic | phlegmatic | pragmatic | traumatic | charismatic |
|-----------|------------|-----------|-----------|-------------|
| eschew | shrew | curfew | overview | purview |

11. a description of the main features of something  _____

12. area of responsibility a person has  _____

13. emotionally shocked  _____

14. law ordering people to stay home at night  _____

15. emphasizing practical results rather than theories _____

16. a bad tempered nagging woman _____

17. having the power to influence and attract people _____

18. mysterious and difficult to understand _____

19. to avoid doing something for moral reasons _____

20. able to be calm in a dangerous situation _____

# WRITING SENTENCES

Use each new word in the box to write an original sentence.

| enigmatic | phlegmatic | pragmatic | traumatic | charismatic |
|-----------|-----------|-----------|-----------|-------------|
| eschew | shrew | curfew | overview | purview |

21. _____

22. _____

23. _____

24. _____

25. _____

26. _____

27. _____

28. _____

29. _____

30. _____

# UNIT 20

## MEMORY TIPS:

Word building with Roots, Prefixes, and Suffixes:

---

| | |
|---|---|
| **fore** | before; as *foreboding* |
| **im** | not; as *imperceptible* |
| **in** | into, in, on; as *intelligible* |
| **ing** | Noun: result of an activity; as *foreboding* |

---

## NEW WORDS

| | | | | |
|---|---|---|---|---|
| fallible | feasible | eligible | imperceptible | intelligible |
| foreboding | cling | fling | offspring | uprising |

**1. FALLIBLE**    ['fæləb(ə)l] *adj.* not perfect and likely to be wrong   **rhyming sound –ible**

We are only human and we are all **fallible**.

*Word Families*: **fallibility** *n.;* **fallibly** *adv.*

**2. feasible**    ['fizəb(ə)l] *adj.* possible or likely to succeed

Whether our plan is **feasible** or not remains to be proved.

*Word Families*: **feasibility** *n.;* **feasibly** *adv.*

**3. eligible**    ['elɪdʒəb(ə)l] *adj.* allowed by rules or laws to do something

If you apply now, you might be **eligible** for a university scholarship.

*Word Families*: **eligibility** *n.;* **eligibly** *adv.*

**4. imperceptible**     [ˌɪmpərˈseptəb(ə)l] *adj.* too slight or gradual to be noticed

Mary's hesitation was almost **imperceptible**.

*Word Families*: **imperceptibility** *n.;* **imperceptibly** *adj.*

**5. intelligible**     [ɪnˈtelɪdʒəb(ə)l] *adj.* clear or simple enough to understand

The language of Darwin was **intelligible** to experts and non-experts alike.

*Word Families*: **intelligibility** *n.;* **intelligibly** *adj.*

**6. FOREBODING** [fɔrˈboʊdɪŋ] *n.* feeling that something bad is about to happen; *adj.* feeling that something bad is going to happen     **rhyming sound -ing**

The little girl felt a gloomy **foreboding** that something was going to go wrong.

*Word Families*: **forebodingly** *adv.*

**7. cling**     [klɪŋ] *v.* to hold onto someone or something tightly

She had to **cling** onto the door handle until the pain passed.

*Word Families*: **clinger** *n.*

**8. fling**     [flɪŋ] *v.* to throw something carelessly; *n.* brief romantic or sexual relationship

She **flung** her arms around my neck and kissed me.

*Word Families*: **flinger** *n.*

**9. offspring**     [ˈɔfˌsprɪŋ] *n. pl.* someone's child or children; something that has developed as a result of something else

The atom bomb is the **offspring** of the twentieth century physics.

**10. uprising**     [ˈʌpˌraɪzɪŋ] *n.* rebellion or revolt

The **uprising** was cracked down by the army.

# SENTENCE COMPLETION

Choose one of the new words to complete each sentence below. Make changes if necessary.

| fallible | feasible | eligible | imperceptible | intelligible |
|----------|----------|----------|---------------|--------------|
| foreboding | cling | fling | offspring | uprising |

1. Japan's productivity has overtaken America in some industries, but elsewhere the United States has _____ on to its lead.

2. By now he was quite aware as to whence this powerful _____ had sprung.

3. Jennifer was now less concerned about her _____ than she had once been.

4. The computer system has proved _____ again and again this month. It's time to get rid of it.

5. The woman claimed that she had a brief _____ with the governor 15 years ago.

6. An _____ gleam of assent twinkled in her eyes.

7. Their proposal for the expansion of the Convention Center sound quite _____.

8. Almost half the population are _____ to vote in today's election

9. All of a sudden, the sailor's wife had a _____ that he would not return this time.

10. She answered with an almost _____ nod of the head.

# DEFINITION MATCHING

Choose one of the new words to match each definition below.

| fallible | feasible | eligible | imperceptible | intelligible |
|----------|----------|----------|---------------|--------------|
| foreboding | cling | fling | offspring | uprising |

11. rebellion or revolt _____

12. possible or likely to succeed _____

13. too slight or gradual to be noticed      _____

14. to throw something carelessly      _____

15. clear or simple enough to understand      _____

16. hold onto someone or something tightly      _____

17. not perfect and likely to be wrong      _____

18. feeling that something bad is going to happen      _____

19. child or children      _____

20. allowed by rules or laws to do something      _____

## WRITING SENTENCES

Use each new word in the box to write an original sentence.

| fallible | feasible | eligible | imperceptible | intelligible |
|----------|----------|----------|---------------|--------------|
| foreboding | cling | fling | offspring | uprising |

21._____

22._____

23._____

24._____

25._____

26._____

27._____

28._____

29._____

30._____

# UNIT 21

## MEMORY TIPS:

Word building with Roots, Prefixes, and Suffixes:

| | |
|---|---|
| **fore** | before; as *forensic* |
| **fort** | strength, strong; as *fortitude* |
| **magn** | great; as *magnitude* |
| **mult** | many; as *multitude* |
| **grat** | pleasing; as *gratitude* |

## NEW WORDS

| forensic | hectic | heretic | lunatic | diplomatic |
|----------|--------|---------|---------|------------|
| fortitude | gratitude | latitude | magnitude | multitude |

**1. FORENSIC**  [fə'renzɪk] *adj.* relating to or connected with a court of law  **rhyming sound –ic**

The robbers of the bank were convicted on **forensic** evidence alone.

*Word Families*: **forensicality** *n.*; **forensically** *adv.*

**2. hectic**  ['hektɪk] *adj.* rushed or busy

Despite her **hectic** work schedule, Jennifer has rarely had any health problems.

*Word Families*: **hectically** *adv.*

**3. heretic**  ['herətɪk] *n.* person who holds unorthodox opinions

He has been called a lunatic, **heretic**, and fascist because of his beliefs.

*Word Families:* **heretically** *adv.*

**4. lunatic**  ['lunətɪk] *adj.* foolish and irresponsible; *n.* foolish and annoying person

The court committed the old man to **lunatic** asylum.

*Word Families:* **lunatically** *adj.*

**5. diplomatic**  [ˌdɪplə'mætɪk] *adj.* of diplomacy; tactful in dealing with people

This shrewd woman is **diplomatic** in almost anything she has her hands on.

*Word Families:* **diplomacy** n.; **diplomatically** *adv.*

**6. FORTITUDE**  ['fɔrtɪˌtud] *n.* courage in adversity or pain  **rhyming sound -itude**

A great leader must possess the qualities of courage, **fortitude**, and charisma.

*Word Families:* **fortitudinous** *adj.*

**7. gratitude**  ['grætɪˌtud] *n.* a feeling of thankfulness or appreciation, as for gifts or favors

I would like to express our sincere **gratitude** to you for your invaluable support.

**8. latitude**  ['lætəˌtud] *n.* an angular distance in degrees north or south of the equator; scope for freedom of action or thought

Lines of equal **latitude** are called parallels.

*Word Families:* **latitudinal** *adj.*

**9. magnitude**  ['mægnəˌtud] *n.* relative importance or size

The seismologist said the recent earthquake had a **magnitude** of 7.

*Word Families:* **magnitudinous** *adj.*

**10. multitude**  ['mʌltɪˌtud] *n.* great number; great crowd

A good marriage can help to cure a **multitude** of indispositions.

*Word Families:* **multitudinous** *adj.*

## SENTENCE COMPLETION

Choose one of the new words to complete each sentence below. Make changes if necessary.

| forensic | hectic | heretic | lunatic | diplomatic |
|----------|--------|---------|---------|------------|
| fortitude | gratitude | latitude | magnitude | multitude |

1. Rulers should always put the interests of the _____ first.

2. There was no lack of gallantry and _____ in this future leader of the nation.

3. We have never understood the _____ of her problem at home.

4. _____ tests showed that the man had been poisoned.

5. The old chemist was regarded as a _____ by the common people in his days.

6. Golden Dragon City lies at a _____ 30 degrees North.

7. For his wife, Helen, Jason is an absolute idiot and _____.

8. On receiving the birthday gift. her eyes were immediately filled with _____.

9. Thomas has had a very _____ schedule for the past few weeks.

10. The two countries were on the point of war because of the _____ tensions.

## DEFINITION MATCHING

Choose one of the new words to match each definition below.

| forensic | hectic | heretic | lunatic | diplomatic |
|----------|--------|---------|---------|------------|
| fortitude | gratitude | latitude | magnitude | multitude |

11. tactful in dealing with people            _____

12. rushed or busy                            _____

13. relative importance or size               _____

14. relating or connected to a court of law _____

15. a feeling of thankfulness or appreciation _____

16. person who holds unorthodox opinions _____

17. scope for freedom of action or thought _____

18. foolish and irresponsible _____

19. great number; great crowd _____

20. courage in adversity or pain _____

## WRITING SENTENCES

Use each new word in the box to write an original sentence.

| forensic | hectic | heretic | lunatic | diplomatic |
|----------|--------|---------|---------|------------|
| fortitude | gratitude | latitude | magnitude | multitude |

21._____

22._____

23._____

24._____

25._____

26._____

27._____

28._____

29._____

30._____

# UNIT 22

## MEMORY TIPS:

Word building with Roots, Prefixes, and Suffixes:

---

| | |
|---|---|
| **ate** | Verb: cause to be; as *fulminate, cultivate, ruminate, discriminate, predominate* |
| **dis** | apart, not**;** as *discriminate* |
| **pre** | before; as *predominate* |

---

## NEW WORDS

| frivolity | banality | brutality | fatality | frugality |
|---|---|---|---|---|
| fulminate | cultivate | ruminate | discriminate | predominate |

**1. FRIVOLITY**   [bɪˈhimɑθ] *n.* silly behavior or attitudes   **rhyming sound –ity**

Her **frivolity** annoys other people in the office.

*Word Families*: **frivolous** *adj.;* **frivolities** *n. pl;* **frivolously** *adv..*

**2. banality**   [bəˈnælɪti] *n.* conventional or dull ordinariness

His ability to utter **banalities** never ceased to amaze others.

*Word Families*: **banal** *adj.*

**3. brutality**   [bruˈtæləti] *n.* extreme violence

Her unforgettable experience of man was of domination and **brutality**.

*Word Families*: **brutal** *adj.;* **brutally** *adv.*

**4. fatality**    [fəˈtæləti] *n.* a death caused by an accident, war, violence, or disease

Scientists are trying to find the means to reduce the **fatality** of heart disease.

*Word Families*: **fatal** *adj;* **fatally** *adv.*

**5. frugality**    [fruˈgælətɪ] *n.* being thrifty

By **frugality** the woman tried to get along with her small salary.

*Word Families*: **frugal** *adj;* **frugally** *adv.*

**6. FULMINATE**    [ˈfʊlmɪˌneɪt] *v.* to speak or write angrily about something    **rhyming**

**sound -ate**

The newspapers **fulminate** against the crimes in the city.

*Word Families*: **fulmination** *n.*

**7. cultivate**    [ˈkʌltɪˌveɪt] *v.* to prepare (land) to grow crops; to develop or

improve something

Thomas has tried very hard to **cultivate** good relations with his colleagues.

*Word Families*: **cultivation** *n.*

**8. ruminate**    [ˈrumɪˌneɪt] *v.* to think about something very seriously

Obsessional personalities commonly **ruminate** excessively about death.

**9. discriminate**    [dɪˈskrɪmɪˌneɪt] *v.* to treat someone unfairly; to recognize the difference

It is hard to **discriminate** the subtle difference between the two qualities.

*Word Families*: **discrimination** *n.*

**10. predominate**    [prɪˈdɑmiˌneɪt] *v.* be the main or dominate element

In older age groups women **predominate** because men tend to die younger.

*Word Families*: **predominant** *adj.;* **predominantly** *adv.*

# SENTENCE COMPLETION

Choose one of the new words to complete each sentence below. Make changes if necessary.

| frivolity | banality | brutality | fatality | frugality |
|-----------|----------|-----------|----------|-----------|
| fulminate | cultivate | ruminate | discriminate | predominate |

1. In this neighborhood immigrants _____ over the natives of the city.

2. Drunk driving _____ have declined more than 10 percent over the past 10 years.

3. We have no right to _____ against others.

4. It all happens with the implacable symmetry and merciless _____ of life.

5. The man accused the police of unwarranted _____ during the riot.

6. The students all _____ against the tuition increase this year.

7. There is a serious message at the core of all this _____ in the city.

8. We should cultivate the good habits of diligence and _____.

9. Mary seems to have spent all her life to _____ her career as a business executive.

10. Those who don't need time to _____ about the meaning of life turn to live longer.

# DEFINITION MATCHING

Choose one of the new words to match each definition below.

| frivolity | banality | brutality | fatality | frugality |
|-----------|----------|-----------|----------|-----------|
| fulminate | cultivate | ruminate | discriminate | predominate |

11. be the main or dominate element _____

12. being thrifty _____

13. extreme violence _____

14. a death caused by an accident, war, or disease     _____

15. to treat someone unfairly     _____

16. conventional or dull ordinariness     _____

17. to speak or write angrily about something     _____

18. silly behavior or attitudes     _____

19. to think about something very carefully     _____

20. to develop or improve something     _____

## WRITING SENTENCES

Use each new word in the box to write an original sentence.

| frivolity | banality | brutality | fatality | frugality |
|-----------|----------|-----------|----------|-----------|
| fulminate | cultivate | ruminate | discriminate | predominate |

21. _____

22. _____

23. _____

24. _____

25. _____

26. _____

27. _____

28. _____

29. _____

30. _____

# UNIT 23

## MEMORY TIPS:

Word building with Roots, Prefixes, and Suffixes:

| | |
|---|---|
| **ag** | do, act; as *agonize* |
| **ize** | Verb: cause; as *galvanize, apprize, downsize, agonize, amortize* |
| **mort** | death; as *amortize* |

## NEW WORDS

| galvanize | aggrandize | agonize | amortize | monopolize |
|---|---|---|---|---|
| garish | parish | relish | embellish | impoverish |

**1. GALVANIZE**   ['gælvə,naɪz] *v.* to stimulate into action; to coat metal with zinc   **rhyming sound –ize**

The tax increase has **galvanized** the business community.

*Word Families*: **galvanization** *n.*

**2. aggrandize**   [ə'græn,daɪz] *v.* to increase the size or scope of something; to make somebody or something seem greater or bigger

The dream of his life is to **aggrandize** the estate of his family.

*Word Families*: **aggrandizement** *n.;* **aggrandizer** *n.*

**3. agonize**   ['ægə,naɪz] v. to spend a long time worrying and being upset about something

The poor woman only made the decision to apply for training after years of **agonizing**.

*Word Families*: **agony** *n.;* **agonizing** *adj.;* **agonizingly** *adv.*

**4. amortize**    ['æmər,taɪz] *v.* to pay off a debt by periodic payments

Our business expenses will have to be **amortized** over a 24 months period.

*Word Families*: **amortization** *n.*

**5. monopolize**    [mə'nɑpə,laɪz] *v.* to have or take exclusive possession of

This company controls so much sugar that it is virtually **monopolizing** the market.

*Word Families*: **monopolization** *n.;* **monopoly** *n.*

**6. GARISH**    ['gerɪʃ] *adj.* very bright and colorful in a ugly way    **rhyming sound -ish**

All around you there seemed to be something glaring, **garish**, rattling.
*Word Families*: **garishness** *n.;* **garishly** *adv.*

**7. parish**    ['perɪʃ] n. an area where it has its own church and clergyman

His preaching was inspiring and well-received in the **parish**.

**8. relish**    ['relɪʃ] *n.* great pleasure and satisfaction; *v.* to get pleasure

I have no **relish** for poor music.

*Word Families*: **relishable** *adj.*

**9. embellish**    [ɪm'belɪʃ] *v.* to make a story more interesting by adding details; to make something more beautiful by decorating

The stern was **embellished** with carvings in red and blue.

*Word Families*: **embellisher** *n.*

**10. impoverish**    [ɪm'pɑvərɪʃ] *v.* to make a country or person very poor

We need to reduce the burden of taxes that **impoverish** the people.
*Word Families*: **impoverishment** *n.*

# SENTENCE COMPLETION

Choose one of the new words to complete each sentence below. Make changes if necessary.

| galvanize | aggrandize | agonize | amortize | monopolize |
|-----------|------------|---------|----------|------------|
| garish | parish | relish | embellish | impoverish |

1. She rejected everything that was _____ and trite.

2. He always _____ the challenge of doing jobs that others turn down.

3. The King sought to _____ himself at the expense of his people.

4. Thy worship does not _____ the world.

5. It has always been a problem to _____ students into studying harder.

6. As usual, Mary _____ the conversation last night.

7. There's no reason to _____ over telling people you're job hunting.

8. I asked him not to _____ the truth with ideas of his own.

9. Jack has decided to _____ the total cost of his car over five years.

10. John became a rector of a small _____ where he ministered for several years.

# DEFINITION MATCHING

Choose one of the new words to match each definition below.

| galvanize | aggrandize | agonize | amortize | monopolize |
|-----------|------------|---------|----------|------------|
| garish | parish | relish | embellish | impoverish |

11. great pleasure and satisfaction _____

12. to pay off a debt by periodic payments _____

13. very bright and colorful in a ugly way _____

14. to worry and being upset about something _____

15. an area that has its own church and clergyman _____

16. to have or take exclusive possession of _____

17. to stimulate into action _____

18. to make a country or people very poor _____

19. to increase the size or scope of something _____

20. to make something more beautiful by decorating _____

## WRITING SENTENCES

Use each new word in the box to write an original sentence.

| galvanize | aggrandize | agonize | amortize | monopolize |
|-----------|-----------|---------|----------|------------|
| garish | parish | relish | embellish | impoverish |

21._____

22._____

23._____

24._____

25._____

26._____

27._____

28._____

29._____

30._____

# UNIT 24

## MEMORY TIPS:

Word building with Roots, Prefixes, and Suffixes:

---

| | |
|---|---|
| **in** | not; as *incongruent* |
| **ious** | characterized by; as *gregarious, hilarious, nefarious, precarious, omnifarious* |
| **loqu** | speak, talk; as *grandiloquent* |
| **omni** | all, every; as *omnifarious* |

---

## NEW WORDS

| grandiloquent | affluent | confluent | effluent | incongruent |
|---|---|---|---|---|
| gregarious | hilarious | nefarious | precarious | omnifarious |

**1. GRANDILOQUENT** [græn'dɪləkwənt] *adj.* expressed in extremely formal language to impress people, and often sound silly   **rhyming sound –ent**

Jenny criticized her colleagues for indulging in **grandiloquent** language.

*Word Families*: **grandiloquence** *n.;* **grandiloquently** *adv.*

**2. affluent**   ['æfluənt] *adj.* rich enough to buy things for pleasure

The lifestyle of the **affluent** has not changed much over the past decade.

*Word Families*: **affluence** *n.;* **affluently** *adv.*

**3. confluent** ['kɑnfluənt] *adj.* flowing together, merging

A **confluent** small - pox had in all directions flowed over his face.

**4. effluent** ['efluənt] *n.* liquid waste such as sewage waste or factory waste

We can see that dangerous **effluent** is poured into the rivers daily.

**5. incongruent** [ɪn'kɑŋgruənt] *adj.* not corresponding in structure or content

His conduct is **incongruent** with our principles.

*Word Families*: **incongruence** *n.;* **incongruently** *adj.*

**6. GREGARIOUS** [grə'geriəs] *adj.* fond of company; (animals) living in flocks    **rhyming sound -ious**

Helen is a **gregarious** and outgoing person.

*Word Families*: **gregariousness** *n.;* **gregariously** *adv.*

**7. hilarious** [hɪ'leriəs] *adj.* extremely funny

I think it would be **hilarious** if we ask Mary to sing in front of others.

*Word Families*: **hilariously** *adv.*

**8. nefarious** [nɪ'feriəs] *adj.* evil or dishonest

That man was a **nefarious** murderer.

*Word Families*: **nefariousness** *n.;* **nefariously** *adv.*

**9. precarious** [prɪ'keriəs] *adj.* likely to change or become dangerous without warning

I am sure you have heard about John's **precarious** lifestyle.

*Word Families*: **precariousness** *n;* **precariously** *adv.*

**10. omnifarious** [ˌɑmnɪ'fɛriəs] *adj.* of all varieties or forms or kinds

With the progressing of modernization of life, **omnifarious** home appliances are put out on the market.

# SENTENCE COMPLETION

Choose one of the new words to complete each sentence below. Make changes if necessary.

| grandiloquent | affluent | confluent | effluent | incongruent |
|---|---|---|---|---|
| gregarious | hilarious | nefarious | precarious | omnifarious |

1. Michael did his research on the _____ use of imagery in modern poetry.

2. When you get into the Target Store, you can see _____ computers and cell phones.

3. All industrial chemical plants produce waste _____.

4. They are _____ birds and feed in flocks.

5. The politician never speaks simply. She is always _____.

6. They put the man under house arrest to some _____ purpose.

7. The party became more _____ when the Hollywood actress arrived.

8. _____ thinking for financial management is highly important for today's decision-makers.

9. Our company's financial situation became _____ last year due to the recession.

10. Cigarette smoking used to be commoner among _____ people.

# DEFINITION MATCHING

Choose one of the new words to match each definition below.

| grandiloquent | affluent | confluent | effluent | incongruent |
|---|---|---|---|---|
| gregarious | hilarious | nefarious | precarious | omnifarious |

11. likely to change or fail _____

12. of all varieties or forms or kinds _____

13. rich enough to buy things for pleasure _____

14. evil or dishonest _____

15. flowing together; merging    _____

16. extremely funny    _____

17. not corresponding in structure or content    _____

18. to use formal language to impress people    _____

19. fond of company    _____

20. liquid waste such as sewage waste    _____

# WRITING SENTENCES

Use each new word in the box to write an original sentence.

| grandiloquent | affluent | confluent | effluent | incongruent |
|---|---|---|---|---|
| gregarious | hilarious | nefarious | precarious | omnifarious |

21._____

22._____

23._____

24._____

25._____

26._____

27._____

28._____

29._____

30._____

# UNIT 25

## MEMORY TIPS:

Word building with Roots, Prefixes, and Suffixes:

---

**be**          make, cause; as *beguile*

**com**        together; as *comprise*

**ex**          out of, from; as *exile*

**ile**         capable of being; as *guile, beguile, exile, profile, pedophile*

---

## NEW WORDS

| guile | beguile | exile | profile | pedophile |
|-------|---------|-------|---------|-----------|
| guise | comprise | demise | reprise | surmise |

**1. GUILE**      [gaɪl] *n.* being good at deceiving people      **rhyming sound –ile**

She persuaded the man to sign the agreement by **guile**.

*Word Families*: **guileful** *adj.;* **guilefully** *adv.*

**2. beguile**     [bɪ'gaɪl] .*v.* to persuade or trick someone into doing something

Her paintings **beguiled** the billionaire of Hong Kong.

*Word Families*: **beguileness** *n.;* **beguiler** *n.;* **beguilingly** *adv.*

**3. exile**       ['ek,saɪl] *n.* prolonged or enforced absence from one's own country

He is now living in **exile** in Paris.

**4. profile** ['proʊ,faɪl] *n.* the description of a person or organization; v. to describe

The newspaper has published a **profile** of the missing girl.

*Word Families*: **profiler** *n.*

**5. pedophile** ['pedəʊ,faɪl] *n.* a man who is sexually attracted to children

It is usually difficult to prevent **pedophiles** from having contacts with children.

*Word Families*: **pedophiles** *n.pl.*

**6. GUISE** ['bɔɪst(ə)rəs] *n.* the way that someone or something appears to people
**rhyming sound -ise**

In this **guise** he gathered information about mutinous and subversive designs.

**7. comprise** [kəm'praɪz] *v.* to consist of two or more things; to form something

The budget proposals **comprise** two parts - expenditure and revenue proposals.

**8. demise** [dɪ'maɪz] *n.* the time when something stops existing; the death of a person

Lack of water will contribute to the plant's **demise**.

**9. reprise** [rɪ'priz] *n.* act of repeating something; v. to do something again

But Britain cannot easily **reprise** its Blair-era identity as the freewheeling California of Europe.

**10. surmise** [sə(r)'maɪz] *v. n.* guess, conjecture

She had a guilty look which immediately roused **surmise** in his mind.


# SENTENCE COMPLETION

Choose one of the new words to complete each sentence below. Make changes if necessary.

| guile | beguile | exile | profile | pedophile |
|-------|---------|-------|---------|-----------|

| guise | comprise | demise | reprise | surmise |
|-------|----------|--------|---------|---------|
|       |          |        |         |         |

1. The thief came into the house under the _____ of a TV repairman.

2. Smoking, rather than genetics, was the cause of his early _____.

3. We love children's innocence and lack of _____.

4. We can see that men still know how to _____ women in today's world.

5. This picture shows the suspect in _____.

6. In some respect, the report is a _____ of previous assessment of the case.

7. The politician returned from _____ last week.

8. He _____ that he had found a way to make millions quickly.

9. No one would hire a _____, and in any case he did not deserve anyone's trust.

10. Women _____ 44% of hospital medical staff.

# DEFINITION MATCHING

Choose one of the new words to match each definition below.

| guile | beguile | exile | profile | pedophile |
|-------|---------|-------|---------|-----------|
| guise | comprise | demise | reprise | surmise |

11. an act of repeating something      _____

12. guess or conjecture      _____

13. persuade or trick someone into doing something    _____

14. the time when something stops existing      _____

15. prolonged or enforced to live in a foreign country _____

16. to consist of two or more things      _____

17. being good at deceiving people        _____

18. a man who is sexually attracted to children        _____

19. description of a person, place, or organization        _____

20. the way someone or something appears to people _____

## WRITING SENTENCES

Use each new word in the box to write an original sentence.

| guile | beguile | exile | profile | pedophile |
|-------|---------|-------|---------|-----------|
| guise | comprise | demise | reprise | surmise |

21._____

22._____

23._____

24._____

25._____

26._____

27._____

28._____

29._____

30._____

# UNIT 26

## MEMORY TIPS:

Word building with Roots, Prefixes, and Suffixes:

---

| less | without, missing; as *hapless, dauntless, reckless, ruthless, relentless* |
| ven | come; as *haven, craven, graven, maven, raven* |

---

## NEW WORDS

| hapless | dauntless | reckless | ruthless | relentless |
|---------|-----------|----------|----------|------------|
| haven | craven | graven | maven | raven |

**1. HAPLESS**  ['hæpləs] *adj.* deserving or inciting pity    **rhyming sound –ess**

All of these people were **hapless** victims of the hurricane.

*Word Families*: **haplessness** *n.;* **haplessly** *adv.*

**2. dauntless**  ['dɔntləs] *adj.* never frightened or worried even by dangerous things

**Dauntless** in spirit, they became even stronger through hardships.

*Word Families*: **dauntlessness** *n.;* **dauntlessly** *adv.*

**3. reckless**  ['rekləs] *adj.* heedless about danger

The man was arrested for his **reckless** driving on the highway.

*Word Families*: **recklessness** *n.;* **recklessly** *adv.*

**4. ruthless**      ['ruθləs] *adj.* pitiless, merciless

On the contrary, she was the most **ruthless** girl I have ever seen.

*Word Families:* **ruthlessness** *n.;* **ruthlessly** *adv.*

**5. relentless**      [rɪ'lentləs] *adj.* never stopping one's attempt to achieve something

He was one of the most **relentless** enemies we have ever had.

*Word Families:* **relentlessness** *n.;* **relentlessly** *adv.*

**6. HAVEN**      ['heɪv(ə)n] *n.* place of safety    **rhyming sound -aven**

If emerging markets are such a safe **haven**, why do investors seem to be panicking?

Cypress Mountain is a **haven** for all kinds of animals.

**7. craven**      ['kreɪv(ə)n] *adj.* not brave

The president of the company condemned the deal as **craven** surrender.

*Word Families:* **cravenness** *n.;* **cravenly** *adv.*

**8. graven**      ['grevən] *adj.* being cut into desired shape;

You should not attempt to mold him into your **graven** image.

**9. maven**      ['meɪvən] *n.* an expert in a particular subject

Carol is a movie **maven** for a popular magazine in Los Angeles.

**10. raven**      ['reɪv(ə)n] *n* .a large bird with shiny black feathers; *adj.* black, shiny, and smooth; *v.* to prey on; to eat greedily

Jenny's charming face was framed with **raven** hair.

*Word Families:* **ravenous** *adj.*

# SENTENCE COMPLETION

Choose one of the new words to complete each sentence below. Make changes if necessary.

| hapless | dauntless | reckless | ruthless | relentless |
|---------|-----------|----------|----------|------------|
|         |           |          |          |            |

| haven | craven | graven | maven | raven |
|-------|--------|--------|-------|-------|

1. A large _____ perched high in the pine near my house.

2. You will be a negotiating _____ if you keep practicing like this.

3. Even though there are myriad hardships and hazards, they can't stop the _____ explorers.

4. His sense of nobility, integrity, and authority left his offspring a _____ effect.

5. The _____ beggar didn't implore Scrooge to bestow anything upon him.

6. James is the one who has given himself up to the _____ pursuit of sensual pleasure.

7. I had no doubt that the _____ fellow would be only too pleased to back out.

8. He is a little bit _____ in his behavior, but you can't help liking him.

9. Manning National Park is truly a _____ for all kinds of wild animals.

10. Michael is not as _____ as he is said to be.

# DEFINITION MATCHING

Choose one of the new words to match each definition below.

| hapless | dauntless | reckless | ruthless | relentless |
|---------|-----------|----------|----------|------------|
| haven | craven | graven | maven | raven |

11. someone who is dazzlingly skilled in a field _____

12. a large black bird with shiny feathers _____

13. being cut into desired shape _____

14. heedless about danger _____

15. not brave _____

16. deserving or inciting pity     _____

17. never stop one's attempt to achieve something     _____

18. place of safety     _____

19. never frightened even by dangerous things     _____

20. pitiless, merciless     _____

# WRITING SENTENCES

Use each new word in the box to write an original sentence.

| hapless | dauntless | reckless | ruthless | relentless |
|---------|-----------|----------|----------|------------|
| haven   | craven    | graven   | maven    | raven      |

21._____

22._____

23._____

24._____

25._____

26._____

27._____

28._____

29._____

30._____

# UNIT **27**

## MEMORY TIPS:

Word building with Roots, Prefixes, and Suffixes:

---

| | |
|---|---|
| **hyper** | too much; as *hypercritical* |
| **hypo** | too little, under; as *hypocritical* |
| **in** | not; as *incredulous* |
| **ous, ious** | having the quality of, relating to; as *hazardous, ignominious, impervious, imperious, incredulous* |

---

## NEW WORDS

| hazardous | imperious | impervious | ignominious | incredulous |
|---|---|---|---|---|
| hypocritical | critical | radical | parasitical | hypercritical |

1. **HAZARDOUS** ['hæzərdəs] *adj.* dangerous (to people's health and safety)   **rhyming sound —ous**

These factories have no way to dispose of the **hazardous** waste they produce.

*Word Families*: **hazardousness** *n.;* **hazardously** *adv.*

2. **imperious** [ɪm'pɪriəs] *adj.* behaving in a proud and confident way

This girl's attitude is **imperious** at times.

*Word Families*: **imperiousness** *n.;* **imperiously** *adv.*

**3. impervious**    [ɪmˈpɜrviəs] *adj.* not affected by something or not seeming to notice

Jenny seemed almost **impervious** to the criticism from others.

*Word Families*: **imperviousness** *n.;* **imperviously** *adv.*

**4. ignominious**    [ˌɪgnəˈmɪniəs] *adj.* very embarrassing

Many people thought that he would be doomed to **ignominious** failure.

**5. incredulous**    [ɪnˈkredʒələs] *adj.* not able to believe something

The pretty girl even gave me an **incredulous** glance.

*Word Families*: **incredulousness** *n.;* **incredulously** *adv.*

**6. HYPOCRITICAL** [ˌhɪpəˈkrɪtɪk(ə)l] *adj.* pretence of having moral principles and beliefs
      **rhyming sound -ical**

It is absolutely **hypocritical** to say one thing but do another.

*Word Families*: **hypocritically** *adv.*

**7. critical**    [ˈkrɪtɪk(ə)l] *adj.* very important or dangerous; fault-finding

It is of **critical** importance to set priorities in what we do.

*Word Families*: **criticism** *n.;* **critically** *adv.*

**8. radical**    [ˈrædɪk(ə)l] *adj.* advocating fundamental change; *n.* person advocating fundamental (political) change

We made a **radical** change in our expansion plan.

*Word Families*: **radicalism** *n.* **radically** *adv.*

**9. parasitical**    [ˌpærəˈsɪtɪkl] *adj.* relating to or caused by parasites; living off another

The young man simply lives a **parasitical** life.

**10. hypercritical**  [ˌhaɪpərˈkrɪtɪk(ə)l] *adj.* tending to criticize a lot in a very unfair way

He is so **hypercritical** that he would not tolerate any mistakes in our essays.


# SENTENCE COMPLETION

Choose one of the new words to complete each sentence below. Make changes if necessary.

| hazardous | imperious | impervious | ignominious | incredulous |
|-----------|-----------|------------|-------------|-------------|
| hypocritical | critical | radical | parasitical | hypercritical |

1.  The country's political system has been _____ to all suggestions of change.

2.  The authorities are considering an airlift if the situation becomes _____ in the region.

3.  A man who is always _____ to others should improve his self-cultivation.

4.  Michael's _____ look made all of us very angry at the party.

5.  Surface water on the highway made driving very _____.

6.  I can't believe that Jennifer is such a _____ girl.

7.  No matter how deep the enmity is and how fierce the revenge is, it is _____ to hurt the innocent people.

8.  There is a political tension between the _____ and conservative politicians.

9.  Dr. Smith is conducting an investigation of the goat's _____ infections in the region.

10. The woman's laughter was so unaffected, so _____, that the officers were impressed.

# DEFINITION MATCHING

Choose one of the new words to match each definition below.

| hazardous | imperious | impervious | ignominious | incredulous |
|-----------|-----------|------------|-------------|-------------|
| hypocritical | critical | radical | parasitical | hypercritical |

11. very embarrassing                          _____

12. claiming to have certain moral principles   _____

13. advocating fundamental change               _____

14. behaving in a proud and confident way _____

15. tending to criticize a lot in a very unfair way _____

16. very important or dangerous _____

17. not affected by something _____

18. not able to believe something _____

19. relating to or caused by parasites _____

20. dangerous, especially to health and safety _____

## WRITING SENTENCES

Use each new word in the box to write an original sentence.

| hazardous | imperious | impervious | ignominious | incredulous |
|---|---|---|---|---|
| hypocritical | critical | radical | parasitical | hypercritical |

21. _____

22. _____

23. _____

24. _____

25. _____

26. _____

27. _____

28. _____

29. _____

30. _____

# UNIT 28

## MEMORY TIPS:

Word building with Roots, Prefixes, and Suffixes:

---

**Able**      able; as *imperturbable, immutable, impalpable, impermeable, ineluctable*

**con**      together; as *concur*

**im, in**      not; as *imperturbable, immutable, impalpable, impermeable, ineluctable*

**cur**      run; as *incur, concur, demur, occur, recur*

---

## NEW WORDS

| imperturbable | immutable | impalpable | impermeable | ineluctable |
|---|---|---|---|---|
| incur | concur | demur | occur | recur |

**1. IMPERTURBABLE** [ˌimpə(r)'tɜr(r)bəb(ə)l] *adj.* always calm and not easily upset  **rhyming sound –able**

Joyce, of course, was cool, aloof, and **imperturbable**.

*Word Families*: **imperturbability** *n.;* **imperturbably** *adv.*

**2. immutable**      [ɪ'mjutəb(ə)l] *adj.* impossible to change; always true, or always the same

Nothing in the world is **immutable**.

*Word Families*: **immutability** *n.;* **immutably** *adv.*

**3. impalpable**      [ɪm'pælpəbəl] *adj.* not being capable of being perceived by the senses

119

The **impalpable** power of faith is beyond our understanding.

*Word Families*: **impalpability** *n.;* **impalpably** *adv.*

4. **impermeable** [ɪmˈpɜrmiəb(ə)l] *adj.* not allowing fluid or gas to pass through it

This Indian canoe is made from an **impermeable** wood.

*Word Families*: **impermeability** *n.*

5. **ineluctable** [ˌɪnɪˈlʌktəb(ə)l] *adj.* impossible to avoid

Those war plans rested on a belief in the **ineluctable** superiority of the offense over the defense.

*Word Families*: **ineluctability** *n.;* **ineluctably** *adv.*

6. **INCUR** [ɪnˈkɜr] *v.* to cause something (unpleasant) to happen; to lose money or

owe money

The government has **incurred** huge debts in recent years.

*Word Families*: **incurrence** *n.*

7. **concur** [kənˈkɜr] *v.* to agree with someone or something

We suggest that you **concur** with us in this matter.

8. **demur** [dɪˈmɜr] *v.* to refuse to do something; *n.* refusal or disagreement

They have accepted the proposal without **demur**.

*Word Families*: **raucousness** *n.;* **raucously** *adv.*

9. **occur** [əˈkɜr] *v.* to happen, especially unexpectedly

The plane crash **occurred** when the crew shut down the wrong engine.

*Word Families*: **occurrence** *n.*

10. **recur** [rɪˈkɜr] *v.* to happen or occur again; to return in thought or speech

Economic crises **recur** periodically.

*Word Families*: **recurrence** *n.*

# SENTENCE COMPLETION

Choose one of the new words to complete each sentence below. Make changes if necessary.

| imperturbable | immutable | impalpable | impermeable | ineluctable |
|---|---|---|---|---|
| incur | concur | demur | occur | recur |

1. The onward march of globalization is, of course, not _____.

2. Her illness is likely to _____ in several years.

3. The man's _____ face was as inexpressive as his rusty clothes.

4. It _____ to me that I could have the ticket sent to me by Federal Express.

5. There is something more fundamental and more _____ at work in our life.

6. Their political views _____ with ours completely.

7. The external layer of the skin is relatively _____ to water.

8. Any cost you _____ on your trip abroad will be reimbursed in full by the company.

9. In the end Nixon accepted our unanimous advice without _____.

10. Our nature is not considered _____, either socially or biologically.


# DEFINITION MATCHING

Choose one of the new words to match each definition below.

| imperturbable | immutable | impalpable | impermeable | ineluctable |
|---|---|---|---|---|
| incur | concur | demur | occur | recur |

11. refusal or disagreement          _____

12. to happen, especially unexpectedly          _____

13. impossible to change          _____

14. to happen or occur again _____

15. to agree with someone or something _____

16. not capable of being perceived by the senses _____

17. to lose money, owe money, or have to pay money _____

18. not allowing liquid or gas to pass through it _____

19. impossible to avoid _____

20. always calm and not easily upset _____

## WRITING SENTENCES

Use each new word in the box to write an original sentence.

| imperturbable | immutable | impalpable | impermeable | ineluctable |
|---|---|---|---|---|
| incur | concur | demur | occur | recur |

21. _____

22. _____

23. _____

24. _____

25. _____

26. _____

27. _____

28. _____

29. _____

30. _____

# UNIT 29

## MEMORY TIPS:

Word building with Roots, Prefixes, and Suffixes:

---

| | |
|---|---|
| **con** | together; as *confer* |
| **fer** | bear, carry; as *infer, confer, defer, refer, transfer* |
| **im, in** | not; as *indigenous, impetuous, innocuous, lugubrious, meretricious* |
| **ous, ious** | characterized by; as *indigenous, impetuous, innocuous, lugubrious, meretricious* |

---

## NEW WORDS

| indigenous | impetuous | innocuous | lugubrious | meretricious |
|---|---|---|---|---|
| infer | confer | defer | refer | transfer |

**1. INDEGENOUS** [ɪnˈdɪdʒənəs] *adj.* born in or natural to a country     **rhyming sound –ous**

Each country has its own **indigenous** cultural traditions and customs.

**2. impetuous**     [ɪmˈpetʃuəs] *adj.* done quickly, without thinking about what the effects will be

Jordon is a young and **impetuous** fellow from Dallas.

*Word Families*: **impetuosity** *n.;* **impetuousness** *n.;* **impetuously** *adv.*

**3. innocuous**  [ɪ'nɑkjuəs]. *adj.* not likely to offend or upset anyone

Even seemingly **innocuous** words are offensive in certain contexts.

*Word Families*: **innocuousness** *n. ;* **innocuously** *adv.*

**4. lugubrious**  [lə'gubriəs] *adj.* looking very sad or serious

These things are charming when one is happy, but **lugubrious** when one is sad.

*Word Families*: **lugubriousness** *n.;* **lugubriously** *adv.*

**5. meretricious**  [ˌmerə'trɪʃəs] *adj.* seeming to be good but not really having any value at all

A wooden building painted to look like marble is **meretricious.**

**6. INFER**  [ɪn'fɜr] *v.* to work out from evidence    **rhyming sound -er**

The police **inferred** that they found her behavior rather suspicious.

*Word Families*: **inference** *n.;* **inferable** *adj.*

**7. confer**  [kən'fɜr] *v.* to discuss together; to grant; to give

An honorary doctorate of law was **conferred** on him by New York University in 1986.

*Word Families*: **conferment** *n.;* **conferral** *n.;* **conferrable** *adj.*

**8. defer**  [dɪ'fɜr] *v.* to delay (something ) until a future time

Customers often **defer** payment as long as possible.

*Word Families*: **deferment** *n.;* **deferral** *n.;* **deferrable** *adj.;* **deferrer** *n.*

**9. refer**  [rɪ'fɜr] *v.* to allude (to); to send (to) for information; be relevant (to)

That is the reason why Marxists **refer** to this kind of movement as scientific socialism.

*Word Families*: **referrer** *n.;* **referable** *adj.*

**10. transfer**  ['trænsfər] *v., n.* to move or send from one person or place to another

The patient was **transferred** to another hospital for immediate operation.

*Word Families*: **transferee** *n.;* **transferor** *n.;* **transferable** *adj.*

# SENTENCE COMPLETION

Choose one of the new words to complete each sentence below. Make changes if necessary.

| indigenous | impetuous | innocuous | lugubrious | meretricious |
|------------|-----------|-----------|------------|--------------|
| infer | confer | defer | refer | transfer |

1.  After the earthquake, the city was full of _____ faces.

2.  In his speech, he _____ to a recent trip to Asia.

3.  Her bedroom was painted in a _____ color.

4.  The Philippines needs capital and technology _____ to help with its economy.

5.  The _____ population in the region is getting smaller with each passing day.

6.  There were a few people Clinton wished to _____ with at the conference.

7.  Young people are usually more _____ than old people.

8.  From what you have said I can _____ that you are doing well in New York.

9.  The question appeared _____ enough, but I still did not trust her.

10. We wish to _____ our decision until next January.


# DEFINITION MATCHING

Choose one of the new words to match each definition below.

| indigenous | impetuous | innocuous | lugubrious | meretricious |
|------------|-----------|-----------|------------|--------------|
| infer | confer | defer | refer | transfer |

11. be relevant (to); to allude to          _____

12. born in or natural to a country          _____

13. to send from one person or place to another    _____

14. done without thinking much about the effects    _____

15. to delay (something) until a future time    _____

16. to grant; to give    _____

17. seeming to be good but not having any value    _____

18. not likely to offend or upset anyone    _____

19. to work out from evidence    _____

20. looking very sad or serious    _____

## WRITING SENTENCES

Use each new word in the box to write an original sentence.

| indigenous | impetuous | innocuous | lugubrious | meretricious |
|------------|-----------|-----------|------------|--------------|
| infer | confer | defer | refer | transfer |

21. _____

22. _____

23. _____

24. _____

25. _____

26. _____

27. _____

28. _____

29. _____

30. _____

# UNIT **30**

## MEMORY TIPS:

Word building with Roots, Prefixes, and Suffixes:

---

| | |
|---|---|
| **con** | together; as *convective* |
| **ic** | of like; as *ironic, demonic, euphonic, harmonic, laconic* |
| **intro** | between, among; as *introspective,* |
| **ive** | relating to; as *introspective, convective, injective, perspective, prospective* |

---

## NEW WORDS

| introspective | connective | perspective | prospective | retrospective |
|---|---|---|---|---|
| ironic | sonic | demonic | harmonic | laconic |

**1. INTROSPECTIVE** [ˌɪntrəˈspektɪv] *adj.* examining your own feelings, thoughts or ideas
      **rhyming sound –ective**

      Satire is a lonely and **introspective** occupation, for nobody can describe a fool to the life without much patient self-inspection.

      *Word Families*: **introspection** *n.* ; **introspectively** *adj.*

**2. connective**     [kəˈnektɪv] *adj.* joining things together; *n.* an instrumentality that connects

      The surgeon cut through **connective** tissue to expose the bone.

**3. perspective**     [pərˈspektɪv] *n.* a way of thinking about something; a view of a large area

      She said that the death of her mother has given her a new **perspective** on life.

**4. prospective**    [prəˈspɛktɪv] *adj.* likely or expected to happen

When Mary's **prospective** employer learned that she had worked abroad, they hired her on the spot.

*Word Families*: **prospectively** *adj.*

**5. retrospective**    [ˌrɛtrəˈspɛktɪv] *adj.* looking back in time; applying from a date in the past

The tax ruling has **retrospective** effect.

*Word Families*: **retrospectively** *adj.*

**6. IRONIC**    [aɪˈrɑnɪk] *adj.* using irony; expressing the opposite of what you really think
**rhyming sound -ic**

The film is more of an **ironic** fantasy than a horror story.

*Word Families*: **ironical** *adj.*

**7. sonic**    [ˈsɔnik] *adj.* relating to sound and sound waves

He activated the door with the miniature **sonic** transmitter.

**8. demonic**    [dɪˈmɑnɪk] *adj.* connected with demons

All of its players are **demonic** and doomed to perish.

*Word Families*: **demonically** *adv.*

**9. harmonic**    [hɑrˈmɑnɪk] *adj.* of harmony

He has been looking for ways to combine **harmonic** and rhythmic

structures.

*Word Families*: **harmonically** *adv.*

**10. laconic**    [ləˈkɑnɪk] *adj.* using very few words

She sent me a **laconic** private message yesterday.

*Word Families*: **laconicism** *n.;* **laconically** *adv.*

# SENTENCE COMPLETION

Choose one of the new words to complete each sentence below. Make changes if necessary.

| introspective | connective | perspective | prospective | retrospective |
|---|---|---|---|---|
| ironic | sonic | demonic | harmonic | laconic |

1. Loans are a little bit easier to come by for _____ homebuyers.

2. My classmates used to call me Dr. Tom Shakespeare at high school, but they were just being _____.

3. A new matching method for _____ pairing is also presented.

4. The evil man seemed to have _____ blood in him.

5. His works expresses an _____ consciousness of individual isolation.

6. A _____ influence pervaded the whole performance.

7. What you call emotion or feeling is the _____ between us.

8. The new aircraft creates a _____ boom.

9. You can get a _____ of the whole city from here.

10. His _____ answers to my request for directions were both unfriendly and abrupt.

# DEFINITION MATCHING

Choose one of the new words to match each definition below.

| introspective | connective | perspective | prospective | retrospective |
|---|---|---|---|---|
| ironic | sonic | demonic | harmonic | laconic |

11. a way of thinking about something    _____

12. using very few words    _____

13. likely or expected to happen    _____

14. expressing the opposite of what you really think _____

15. examining your own feelings, thoughts or ideas _____

16. looking back in time _____

17. relating to sound and sound waves _____

18. of harmony _____

19. an instrumentality that connects _____

20. connected with demons _____

# WRITING SENTENCES

Use each new word in the box to write an original sentence.

| introspective | connective | perspective | prospective | retrospective |
|---|---|---|---|---|
| ironic | sonic | demonic | harmonic | laconic |

21. _____

22. _____

23. _____

24. _____

25. _____

26. _____

27. _____

28. _____

29. _____

30. _____

# ANSWER KEY

## UNIT 1

### SENTENCE COMPLETION

1. ransack 2.crack 3. temptation 4. ration 5. inflation 6. aback 7. rack 8. aberration 9. abbreviation 10. counterattack

### DEFINITION MATCHING

11. aberration 12. crack 13. abbreviation 14. rack 15. aback 16. ransack 17. temptation 18. ration 19. counterattack 20. inflation

### WRITING SENTENCES

Answers will vary based on students' personal experiences.

## UNIT 2

### SENTENCE COMPLETION

1. abhor 2.decor 3. ambassador 4. abet 5. cadet 6. mentor 7. beget 8. asset 9. metaphor 10. regret

### DEFINITION MATCHING

11. decor 12. regret 13. metaphor 14. abhor 15. ambassador 16. cadet 17. beget 18. mentor 19. abet 20. asset

### WRITING SENTENCES

Answers will vary based on students' personal experiences.

## UNIT 3

### SENTENCE COMPLETION

1. homicide 2.prospect 3. neglect 4. abide 5. subsided 6. collide 7. confided 8. defect 9. abject 10. affects

### DEFINITION MATCHING

11. collide 12. neglect 13. confide 14. prospect 15. affect 16. abject 17. subside 18. homicide 19. abide 20. defect

**WRITING SENTENCES**

Answers will vary based on students' personal experiences.

# UNIT 4

## SENTENCE COMPLETION

1. abominate 2.matriculate 3. accelerate 4. excoriate 5. accumulate 6. abjure 7. immature 8. obscure 9. conjure 10. endure

## DEFINITION MATCHING

11. accumulate 12. immature 13. matriculate 14. abominate 15. obscure 16. accelerate 17. excoriate 18. endure 19. conjure 20. abjure

## WRITING SENTENCES

Answers will vary based on students' personal experiences.

# UNIT 5

## SENTENCE COMPLETION

1. detain 2.abstain 3. diffuse 4. constrain 5. profuse 6. abstruse 7. recluse 8. domain 9. effuse 10. refrain

## DEFINITION MATCHING

11. diffuse 12. refrain 13. detain 14. abstruse 15.constrain 16. effuse 17. recluse 18. abstain 19. profuse 20. domain

**WRITING SENTENCES**

Answers will vary based on students' personal experiences.

# UNIT 6

## SENTENCE COMPLETION

1. escalate 2.serenade 3. promenade 4. accentuate 5. escapade 6. accolade 7. correlate 8. adumbrated 9. centigrade 10. allocate

## DEFINITION MATCHING

11. correlate 12. serenade 13. promenade 14. adumbrate 15.centigrade 16. allocate 17. escapade 18. accentuate 19. accolade 20. escalate

## WRITING SENTENCES

Answers will vary based on students' personal experiences.

# UNIT 7

## SENTENCE COMPLETION

1. manipulating 2.effervescing 3. confederate 4. acquiesced 5. obsolesced 6. substantiate 7. incorporate 8. deliquesces 9. evanesced 10. amalgamate

## DEFINITION MATCHING

11. obsolesce 12. confederate 13. evanesce 14. incorporate 15. deliquesce 16. manipulate 17. substantiate 18. acquiesce 19. amalgamate 20. effervesce

## WRITING SENTENCES

Answers will vary based on students'

COLUMBIA 1000 WORDS YOU MUST KNOW FOR GRE

personal experiences.

# UNIT 8

## SENTENCE COMPLETION

1. retaliate 2.intoxicate 3. ambivalent 4. degenerate 5. prevalent 6. solvent 7. ameliorate 8. indigent 9. conglomerate 10. pungent

## DEFINITION MATCHING

11. pungent 12. conglomerate 13. intoxicate 14. indigent 15. prevalent 16. retaliate 17. solvent 18. ameliorate 19. degenerate 20. ambivalent

## WRITING SENTENCES

Answers will vary based on students' personal experiences.

# UNIT 9

## SENTENCE COMPLETION

1. malicious 2.judicious 3. officious 4. loquacious 5. vicious 6. capacious 7. auspicious 8. rapacious 9. sagacious 10. audacious

## DEFINITION MATCHING

11. judicious 12. rapacious 13. officious 14. audacious 15. sagacious 16. vicious 17. capacious 18. malicious 19. auspicious 20. loquacious

## WRITING SENTENCES

Answers will vary based on students' personal experiences.

# UNIT 10

## SENTENCE COMPLETION

1. boisterous 2.sloth 3. grievous 4. zealous 5. behemoth 6. raucous 7. broth 8. wroth 9. sumptuous 10. moth's

## DEFINITION MATCHING

11. sumptuous 12. sloth 13. boisterous 14. broth 15. behemoth 16. wroth 17. zealous 18. moth 19. grievous 20. raucous

## WRITING SENTENCES

Answers will vary based on students' personal experiences.

# UNIT 11

## SENTENCE COMPLETION

1. burlesque 2.forecast 3. statuesque 4. sculpturesque 5. have blasted 6. grotesque 7. aghast 8. picturesque 9. bombast 10. iconoclast

## DEFINITION MATCHING

11. picturesque 12. statuesque 13. forecast 14. grotesque 15. burlesque 16. bombast 17. iconoclast 18. sculpturesque 19. blast 20. aghast

## WRITING SENTENCES

Answers will vary based on students' personal experiences.

# UNIT 12

## SENTENCE COMPLETION

1. billow 2.burrow 3. tarnish 4. escrow 5. burnish 6. furnished 7. garnish 8. marrow 9. anguish 10. shallow

## DEFINITION MATCHING

11. tarnish 12. shallow 13. furnish 14. marrow 15. escrow 16. burnish 17. billow 18. anguish 19. burrow 20. garnish

## WRITING SENTENCES

Answers will vary based on students' personal experiences.

# UNIT 13

## SENTENCE COMPLETION

1. licentious 2.sententious 3. appeal 4. zealous 5. congeal 6. ordeal 7. abstentious 8. healed 9. contentious 10. conceal

## DEFINITION MATCHING

11. pretentious 12. contentious 13. heal 14. sententious 15. abstentious 16. conceal 17. licentious 18. congeal 19. appeal 20. ordeal

## WRITING SENTENCES

Answers will vary based on students' personal experiences.

# UNIT 14

## SENTENCE COMPLETION

1. converged 2.submerge 3. obscene 4. diverge 5. gene 6. merge 7. hygiene 8. contravene 9. emerge 10. serene

## DEFINITION MATCHING

11. submerge 12. obscene 13. diverge 14. gene 15. emerge 16. serene 17. merge 18. contravene 19. converge 20. hygiene

## WRITING SENTENCES

Answers will vary based on students' personal experiences.

# UNIT 15

## SENTENCE COMPLETION

1. mischievous 2.exaggerates 3. dubious 4. affiliate 5. odious 6. copious 7. promulgate 8. expurgated 9. corroborate 10. commodious

## DEFINITION MATCHING

11. exaggerate 12. affiliate 13. odious 14. dubious 15. promulgate 16. commodious 17. corroborate 18. expurgate 19. copious 20. mischievous

## WRITING SENTENCES

Answers will vary based on students' personal experiences.

# UNIT 16

## SENTENCE COMPLETION

1. promissory 2.reproachable 3. cursory 4. conservatory 5. unbearable 6. censurable 7. mandatory 8. culpable 9. observatory 10. blamable

## DEFINITION MATCHING

11. observatory 12. reproachable 13. conservatory 14. culpable 15. promissory 16. blamable 17. cursory 18. censurable 19. mandatory 20. unbearable

**WRITING SENTENCES**

Answers will vary based on students' personal experiences.

## UNIT 17

### SENTENCE COMPLETION

1. sycophancy 2.obsolete 3. necromancy 4. deplete 5. fancy 6. replete 7. concrete 8. discrepancy 9. discrete 10. chancy

### DEFINITION MATCHING

11. sycophancy 12. necromancy 13. deplete 14. chancy 15. fancy 16. concrete 17. replete 18. discrepancy 19. discrete 20. obsolete

### WRITING SENTENCES

Answers will vary based on students' personal experiences.

## UNIT 18

### SENTENCE COMPLETION

1. interface 2.abate 3. retrace 4. efface 5. elucidate 6. conflate 7. aerospace 8. rebate 9. disgrace 10. stagnate

### DEFINITION MATCHING

11. stagnate 12. retrace 13. rebate 14. conflate 15. efface 16. elucidate 17. abate 18. aerospace 19. disgrace 20. interface

### WRITING SENTENCES

Answers will vary based on students' personal experiences.

## UNIT 19

### SENTENCE COMPLETION

1. overview 2.enigmatic 3. purview 4. charismatic 5. pragmatic 6. shrew 7. eschew 8. phlegmatic 9. curfew 10. traumatic

### DEFINITION MATCHING

11. overview 12. purview 13. traumatic 14. curfew 15. pragmatic 16. shrew 17. charismatic 18. enigmatic 19. eschew 20. phlegmatic

### WRITING SENTENCES

Answers will vary based on students' personal experiences.

## UNIT 20

### SENTENCE COMPLETION

1. clung 2.uprising 3. offspring 4. fallible 5. fling 6. intelligible 7. feasible 8. eligible 9. foreboding 10. imperceptible

### DEFINITION MATCHING

11. uprising 12. feasible 13. imperceptible 14. fling 15. intelligible 16. cling 17. fallible 18. foreboding 19. offspring 20. eligible

### WRITING SENTENCES

Answers will vary based on students' personal experiences.

## UNIT 21

### SENTENCE COMPLETION

1. multitude 2.fortitude 3. magnitude 4.
   Forensic 5. heretic 6. latitude 7. lunatic
   8. gratitude 9. hectic 10. diplomatic

## DEFINITION MATCHING

11. diplomatic 12. hectic 13. magnitude 14.
    forensic 15. gratitude 16. heretic 17.
    latitude 18. lunatic 19. multitude 20.
    fortitude

## WRITING SENTENCES

Answers will vary based on students'
personal experiences.

# UNIT 22

## SENTENCE COMPLETION

1. predominate 2.fatalities 3. discriminate
   4. banality 5. brutality 6. fulminated 7.
   frivolity 8. frugality 9. cultivate 10.
   ruminate

## DEFINITION MATCHING

11. predominate 12. frugality 13. brutality
    14. fatality 15. discriminate 16. banality
    17. fulminate 18. frivolity 19. ruminate
    20. cultivate

## WRITING SENTENCES

Answers will vary based on students'
personal experiences.

# UNIT 23

## SENTENCE COMPLETION

1. garish 2.relishes 3. aggrandize 4.
   impoverish 5. galvanize 6. monopolized
   7. agonize 8. embellish 9. amortize 10.
   parish

## DEFINITION MATCHING

11. relish 12. amortize 13. garish 14.
    agonize 15. parish 16. monopolize 17.
    galvanize 18. impoverish 19. aggrandize
    20. embellish

## WRITING SENTENCES

Answers will vary based on students'
personal experiences.

# UNIT 24

## SENTENCE COMPLETION

1. incongruent 2.omnifarious 3. effluent 4.
   gregarious 5. grandiloquent 6. nefarious
   7. hilarious 8. confluent 9. precarious
   10. affluent

## DEFINITION MATCHING

11. precarious 12. omnifarious 13. affluent
    14. nefarious 15. confluent 16. hilarious
    17. incongruent 18. grandiloquent 19.
    gregarious 20. effluent

## WRITING SENTENCES

Answers will vary based on students'
personal experiences.

# UNIT 25

## SENTENCE COMPLETION

1. guise 2.demise 3. guile 4. beguile 5.
   profile 6. reprise 7. exile 8. surmise 9.
   pedophile 10. comprise

## DEFINITION MATCHING

11. reprise 12. surmise 13. beguile 14.
    demise 15. exile 16. comprise 17. guile
    18. pedophile 19. profile 20. guise

**WRITING SENTENCES**

Answers will vary based on students'
personal experiences.

# UNIT 26

### SENTENCE COMPLETION

1. raven 2.maven 3. dauntless 4. graven 5.
hapless 6. relentless 7. craven 8.
reckless 9. haven 10. ruthless

### DEFINITION MATCHING

11. maven 12. raven 13. graven 14.
reckless 15. craven 16. hapless 17.
relentless 18. haven 19. dauntless 20.
ruthless

### WRITING SENTENCES

Answers will vary based on students'
personal experiences.

# UNIT 27

### SENTENCE COMPLETION

1. impervious 2.critical 3. hypercritical 4.
imperious 5. hazardous 6. hypocritical 7.
ignominious 8. radical 9. parasitical 10.
incredulous

### DEFINITION MATCHING

11. ignominious 12. hypocritical 13.
radical 14. imperious 15. hypercritical
16. critical 17. impervious 18.
incredulous 19. parasitical 20. hazardous

### WRITING SENTENCES

Answers will vary based on students'
personal experiences.

# UNIT 28

### SENTENCE COMPLETION

1. ineluctable 2.recur 3. imperturbable 4.
occurred 5. impalpable 6. concur 7.
impermeable 8. incur 9. demur 10.
immutable

### DEFINITION MATCHING

11. demur 12. occur 13. immutable 14.
recur 15. concur 16. impalpable 17.
incur 18. impermeable 19. ineluctable
20. imperturbable

### WRITING SENTENCES

Answers will vary based on students'
personal experiences.

# UNIT 29

### SENTENCE COMPLETION

1. lugubrious 2.refer 3. meretricious 4.
transfer 5. indigenous 6. confer 7.
impetuous 8. infer 9. innocuous 10.
defer

### DEFINITION MATCHING

11. refer 12. indigenous 13. transfer 14.
impetuous 15. defer 16. confer 17.
meretricious 18. innocuous 19. infer 20.
lugubrious

### WRITING SENTENCES

Answers will vary based on students'
personal experiences.

# UNIT 30

## SENTENCE COMPLETION

1. prospective 2.ironic 3. harmonic 4.
   demonic 5. introspective 6. retrospective
   7. connective 8. sonic 9. perspective 10.
   laconic

## DEFINITION MATCHING

11. perspective 12. laconic 13. prospective
    14. ironic 15. introspective 16.
    retrospective 17. sonic 18. harmonic 19.
    connective 20. demonic

## WRITING SENTENCES

Answers will vary based on students'
   personal experiences.

# WORD INDEX

This index lists 300 absolutely essential GRE key words appeared in this book. You may use the list as a dictionary to find out the definitions, sample sentences, and the uses of each word to help you review what you have learned and boost your retention.

---

## B

# C

Cadet  15

Capacious  43

Censurable  71

Centigrade  31

Chancy  75

Charismatic  83

Cling  87

Collide  19

Commodious  67

Comprise  107

Conceal  59

Concrete  75

Concur  119

Confederate  35

Confer  123

Confide  19

Conflate  79

Confluent  103

Congeal  59

Conglomerate  39

Conjure  23

Connective  127

Conservatory  71

Constrain  27

Contentious  59

Contravene  63

Converge  63

Copious  67

Correlate  31

Corroborate  67

Counterattack  11

Crack  11

Craven  111

Critical  115

Culpable  71

Cultivate  95

Curfew  83

Cursory  71

# D

# E

## S

## T

## U

# ACKNOWLEDGMENTS

The author would like to thank his colleagues and students for their invaluable assistance in bringing this book to life.

**The author and publisher are grateful to those who have made this publication possible by providing all kinds of support from editing, graphic design, and proof-reading. Efforts have been made to identify the source of materials used in this book, however, it has not always been possible to identify the sources of all the materials used, or to trace the copyright holders. If any omissions are brought to our attention, we will be happy to include the appropriate acknowledgments on reprinting.**

# ABOUT THE AUTHOR

Dr. Richard Lee is a professor of English and distinguished publishing scholar with numerous books published under his name. His books are available on Amazon, other online stores, and in bookstores worldwide. He pursued his doctoral education at the University of Rochester in New York and the University of British Columbia and received his Ph.D. in English.